THE
HOW TO
COLLECT
ANYTHING
BOOK

Also by SYLVIA O'NEILL DORN
The Insider's Guide to Antiques, Art and Collectibles

THE HOW TO COLLECT ANYTHING BOOK

TREASURE TO TRIVIA

Sylvia O'Neill Dorn

DOUBLEDAY & COMPANY, INC.

Garden City, New York   *1976*

ISBN: 0-385-09824-3

Library of Congress Catalog Card Number 75-14814
Copyright © 1976 by Sylvia O'Neill Dorn

For my father, Albert Arpad Schwartz,
who taught us that the best is none too good for all;
and for my mother, Leona née Newberger,
who taught us to perceive that best is most beautiful.

❲ CONTENTS

⟮ PREFACE

Except for those Spartan and disciplined souls who harbor no object not strictly utilitarian on their premises, we all recognize a bit of the packrat in ourselves, especially if we respond to the appeal of antiques and other collectibles and consider ourselves antiquers, or that new genus of sporadic collectors known as freakers, who fancy aspects of popular culture.

We note our random acquisitions, more or less neatly strewn, stacked, or possibly packed away, and indulgently or sternly resolve to desist from further acquisitions and even to sell or otherwise dispose of once irresistible temptations.

What we may not observe is the latent supercollector who also resides within us. This alter ego to the packrat could accomplish a lot more than arouse guilt feelings, if given a chance.

Like the supercollectors we read about, whose collections make headline news when burglarized, auctioned, otherwise sold, donated, or bequeathed, we too can have the profitable, creatively satisfying, and personally enriching achievement of forming a real collection, within our means and suited to our own life styles.

The purpose of this book is to illustrate that all this is possible on whatever scale you choose, and that in addition, it is more rewarding to be even a modest collector than what chess players call a *patzer* and dealers call a *schlepper*, one who just fools around and gets nowhere.

The collector is a selector, who by choosing and assembling objects to illustrate some interesting, remarkable, piquant, or even poignant aspect of life, arouses wonder, that marvelous stretching, soaring of the imagination, which enriches our capacity to function as human beings and subtly contributes to an affirmation of life. Forming a collection can clarify your vision, give you perspective, and enlarge your humanity.

Admittedly, such collections as Disneyana, ironstone china, vintage radios, clothespins, paperweights, or toy trains would not be on a par with J. Pierpont Morgan's collection of medieval treasures, John D. Rockefeller III's collection of oriental art, or Mr. and Mrs. Charles Wrightsman's collection of French decorative arts. Yet they may share with them a basic formula that can be analyzed and tailored to help in the formation of any kind of collection. Whether they consist of "new antiques," classic antiques, fine, folk, or primitive art, whether of offbeat or traditional collectibles, well-formed collections can be valid, venturesome, and with an adherence to guidelines and standards, important and valuable.

It is noteworthy that those who themselves have formed fine collections are the first to appreciate the efforts of others. Ironically, those who would have the most to gain by understanding how to form a collection are usually so dazzled by the sheer glamour of highly heralded collections that they fail to grasp their essential structure. Too often the skills that create a collection are considered inherent in experts, whether as connoisseurs, dealers, or scholars, and beyond the capacity of a layman or hobbyist. Even those who recognize that a collection is a group of objects gathered with a plan, stop there.

Yet that whole fascinating territory of the nature of such plans, their advantages, purposes, and implementation; the choice of subjects, classification, and research; of buying and selling; and of display and protection of collections is no sacred precinct, open only to supercollectors. Nor does it require any special background. In this era of the blue-collar collector, those with wit as well as wealth should have access to it, and this primer invites them to note that one horseshoe is lucky, but a carload is junk!

THE
HOW TO
COLLECT
ANYTHING
BOOK

CHAPTER 1

THE ADVANTAGES OF FORMING A COLLECTION

(GREATER THAN THE SUM OF ITS PARTS
(COLLECTING LENDS ENHANCEMENT
(TO EACH ONE'S OWN
(FORESIGHT IS FARSIGHTED
(FEELING THE WAY   (ON THE ALERT
(ODDITIES ATTRACT   (CONTINUING REWARDS
(HAPPILY HOOKED   (OUT OF THIS WORLD
(COLLECT TO SURVIVE!

MILLIONS OF PEOPLE are presently collecting, but comparatively few are forming collections. It seems a pity, because for about the same amount of money and a little more energy they might have advantages and pleasures far beyond the agreeable diversion they now enjoy as they acquire antiques, art, or other collectibles on a piecemeal basis. They might also avoid some of their problems as custodians of whatever cumbersome miscellany they have accumulated as antiquers, shoppers, heirs, investors, or merely hopeful bargain hunters.

It may well be that among those possessions is the nucleus of a true collection. And those who are presently spending modest sums could be forming collections that did not require much more; those whose expenditures are larger might set their sights with more ambition. As in other matters, rich is better than poor if you want costly things, but there's something in collecting for everyone and there is always room for the collector without money to come up with the definitive collection of safety pins, Dixie cup lids, or pawn tickets, all of which are winning respected places in the collecting spectrum.

⟨ GREATER THAN THE SUM
OF ITS PARTS

Hearing only how others have been richly rewarded by investment in collecting, the hapless individual who takes pictures, antiques, books, or other collectibles to market, to receive only a fraction of their retail or advertised value, often less than they cost, marvels at the disparity, wondering at its cause. Much of it can be attributed to the weakness of an amateur pitted against a professional system. By forming a collection, an individual gains experience and knowledge that equips and arms, and the collection itself has increased potential return because the whole is greater than the sum of its parts.

Essentially, that is what "supercollector" knows and acts upon. And while the spotlight rests on the Norton Simons, Robert Sculls, and Joseph Hirshhorns, more modest supercollectors form their varied collections quietly, industriously, even zealously, and if they too have built cohesive, unified collections, the net worth of the collections will also have grown.

There are exceptions. History records some who have been impoverished by obsession with collecting, and experience teaches the importance of taking adequate precautions at the time of disposal. However, a well-planned collection seldom fails to reward and enrich its creator.

⟨ COLLECTING LENDS ENHANCEMENT

By its very definition, a collection is self-enhancing. A collection is a varying number of diverse objects that have been selected by plan for the purpose of expressing a viewpoint about its components.

Your household button box may include some unusual examples, but it will not qualify as a collection. On the other hand, a selective assortment of buttons, possibly no single one exceptional, will do so. In forming a collection of plastic Art Deco buttons, a collector uses intrinsically negligible material, but in illustrating the variety of designs, sizes, and shapes, creates a whole that is of greater worth than its individual components.

An individual metal match safe in the form of an animal is a clever little curio, but when it becomes part of a collection, literally a zoo of match safes, each figure by contrast and variation enhances the others. Together they all become more desirable, interesting, and valuable than they were separately.

This is also true of intrinsically valuable collections of jade carvings, masterpiece paintings, or rare coins. In an outstanding collection, each object takes on greater importance within the framework of the relationship.

Having once been part of a well-known collection, the object carries this association as part of its dossier, and even when scattered or sold, reflects it in its value as "ex: collection of . . ."

As an advantage for those without superpurses, the commonplace item reflects a greater proportionate value increase than does the rare and costly one. On the other hand, a ten-time escalation from five to fifty dollars is gratifying, but not as likely to enrich as that merely doubling from one hundred thousand dollars to two hundred thousand dollars!

With hindsight, those who have spent few or many years involved on the perimeters of the collecting scene almost unanimously regret that they did not start to form a planned collection at the outset. This is not only because of the comparative bargains available (or so it seems to every succeeding generation) but also because whatever pleasure they did take in browsing and buying would have been heightened by the satisfaction of having produced an original creation.

❲ TO EACH ONE'S OWN

Each collection has a personalized form, designed by its purpose and the collector's capacity and limitations. Nutcrackers, cookbooks, toys, quillwork, vintage radios, and laces have been shaped into collections of consequence, stature, and value because their creators employ the methods and techniques of experts who form famous collections of Byzantine icons or medieval sculptures. The range of material suitable for forming collections is endless, and the possible themes are as varied as the ideas about them. No two collections ever need be alike, as each reflects the influences and circumstances of different lives and outlooks.

❲ FORESIGHT IS FARSIGHTED

In addition to the greater potential profitability of the planned collection, many other advantages accrue to the individual who decides to embark on such a project.

The very fact that a collection requires a plan is a built-in advantage. Additions are given forethought; unexpected and random temptations are screened by supercollectors as though they were passing on new members for an exclusive club. As the outlines of a collection are drawn, each object is considered for its potential

as well as current contribution. Fewer regrets or errors in judgment result, which the lady who collects carousel animals and has
twenty of them in her fourteen-room home finds gratifying.

A program for acquisition brings out the reality of limitations as
well as the hopes and dreams of collectors. Budget, storage space,
life style, even climate must be considered. A large income en-
tailed with heavy obligations may not offer an adequate budget
for a project that a much smaller income frugally assessed might
well finance.

❮ FEELING THE WAY

"Handle at your own risk," as lettered in shops and at shows, may
not completely foreclose, but it will inhibit the kind of close study
possible to the owner of a collection in formation. Close examination and comparison make more experts than any other forms of
study, and the frequent handling of a collection—the opportunity
to feel textures and compare colors, form, and finish—will
heighten discrimination. Familiarity of this kind always breeds
respect for quality, the mark of a successful collector.

In ancient Rome, collectors used to sniff proffered bronzes,
claiming that Corinthian pieces, the most treasured, had a distinctive odor. Stitch sizes in quilts, depths of hallmarks, the feel of
porcelain—these are telltale signs to those who by constant handling develop areas of heightened sensitivity and sensibility.

❮ ON THE ALERT

Spotting fakes—the skill that collectors prize almost as much as
recognizing quality—is best developed by the experience of forming a collection. Certainly the ability to see flaws and otherwise
avoid traps is finely honed in this fashion and is a valuable by-
product of any collecting project. Nobody can know all about everything, but you can get to know a lot about a specialty; thus
specialists are less likely to be cheated.

Limited-edition advertisements and "guarantees" are sometimes
in effect contracts, and require that the purchaser have the skill

of a lawyer reading the small type in an insurance policy or lease. The ability to evaluate such mass-produced "custom" collecting offers comes with the experience of forming an individual and creative collection. It is the best antidote to the barrage of phony enticements directed at naïve victims.

Learning is easiest where there is most incentive; that of forming a collection is enormous. Internationally recognized scholars in a field will defer to the opinions of unschooled collectors who carve out their niches of authority. High school dropouts who collect coins will rattle off seriatim, names of nineteenth-century U. S. Mint directors unknown to historians.

In addition, concentration develops familiarity with periodicals, books, price guides, research facilities, exhibitions, and shows unknown to the casual collector. It also leads to club membership, travel, mail-order buying and selling, and generally broadened horizons. Collectors have been brought together by the long arm of a mutual interest to share information about refinishing, repair facilities, or confidences about the reliability and integrity of dealers, appraisers, and auctioneers. Whether or not collectors become close friends, and often they do not (competition in a specialty can be fierce), awareness and observation of rival collections can be productive.

⟪ ODDITIES ATTRACT

A bonus for forming an unusual collection is to be found in the response of many friendly folk, who on learning that an individual is acquiring fly whisks, cast-iron bottle openers, or carpet sweepers, will go out of the way to extend themselves with information, leads, and unusual examples. This kind of assistance is showered on those with odd and appealing specialties, but often anyone who is known to be a specialist collector will profit from such goodwill.

Not only such friendly assistance from the public, but peer judgment is another advantage of specialization. At a certain level, camaraderie, even an insiders' grapevine, develop between dealers and advanced collectors. Dealers will sometimes identify with the formation of a collection; this is a circumstance devoutly to be wished, and may result in advice, first choice, and possibly an extension of credit as well.

❪ CONTINUING REWARDS

Even if the collector has retired from business and lacks enough income to continue to make outright purchases for the collection, its advantages continue. Research, culling, and refining by trading and swapping assure the retiree of continued participation, and at the very least they guarantee exercise of energies and mental powers. Above all, they offer involvement in a creative aspect of life that can be modified according to circumstances. The greater the identification with the collection during the active preretirement life, the greater the reward. Such collectors hardly have to change gears, as they earn their greatest profit from having invested themselves.

For many there is also a possible use of the nest egg that the collection represents as capital. A degree of comfort in later years from the sale of part or the whole of a collection has been known to make up for the loss of the most cherished treasures.

❪ HAPPILY HOOKED

No matter how materially oriented the collector is at the start, and no matter how concerned with price and profitability, there is usually some place along the way in the ongoing process of forming a collection that becomes a point of no return. When involvement with the design of the project, delight in search and research, sensuous pleasure in handling and arranging combine to give creative satisfaction, that collector has been hooked. Addiction to the highs of acquisition has been achieved, and with it a capacity to rebound from the lows of failure and disappointment. Perhaps the beginning was made in cold blood, purely as a business investment, and though some, inspired solely by speculation, fall by the wayside, others respond to the compulsion and go on to truly creative collecting.

(OUT OF THIS WORLD

The collector arranging and assorting valued treasures has been likened to the child at play, and indeed it has been suggested that the activity is a playful release for the adult retreating from the tensions of daily life. Inside this world it is morally acceptable to be hedonistic, concerned only with personal satisfactions, a relatively rare territory for most responsible people.

Specialist collectors of miniatures agree that they especially enjoy the sense of power and authority they can exercise over their little empires, noting that it compensates for their sense of helplessness in the affairs of the larger world. The probability is that they recognize their own feelings because of the easy logic of the comparison. Actually, all collectors have this sense of control over their collections and find in it refuge and the peace of a well-ordered world, lacking elsewhere.

(COLLECT TO SURVIVE!

Rising above material, emotional, and psychological aspects, a more powerful advantage, reaching into the essential nature of humanity, has recently been related to our activities as collectors.

In an era replete with negative tidings about the human race and its prospects, those interested in collecting will be heartened by the news that at least this particular activity on the increase in "advanced" societies is more useful than hitherto believed.

Research indicates that collecting is not a mere indulgence, but has contributed to the ongoing development of the human as a thinking animal from earliest times, and in addition, like sex, became pleasurable because it was necessary for survival.

Scientists led by Alexander Marshak have discovered that at least thirty-five thousand years ago, after marking notations about the movement of the moon and other natural phenomena on stones and bones, our ancestors collected and treasured this earliest art, which was also science, creating cults and rituals and shaping civilization in the process.

Collecting and classifying information or objects are procedures that reduce the necessity to constantly collate each fact, and by reducing the "thought load," allow quick transference of information from one situation to another. Selective acquisition expands the capacity of the mind, and for that reason still plays a role in our development.

This has a special importance in these times. As our internal computers are displaced by technicians and electronic computers, they may atrophy like the appendix. We need to exercise both selection and discrimination as our options are narrowed about us by prepackaged and preselected food, clothing, entertainment, and ideas. Ironically, the commercial effort to introduce mass prepackaged collecting via "limited editions" only underscores the advantages of forming an original, creative collection.

For over two thousand years, since it became fashionable in ancient Rome, collecting art, antiques, natural, and man-made curiosities and similar treasures has been considered an elite activity—with all due gratitude rendered to the rich and powerful for their donations to public institutions, the taint of self-indulgence, avarice, greed, and ambition for status and power were believed to have been overriding considerations in their pursuit of treasure and formation of collections.

Now, in the first major turnabout in twenty centuries, when despite commercial exploitation, collecting has entered a democratic phase, with popular if not mass interest contributing aspects of earlier, more elemental and even primitive values, reconsideration and possibly rehabilitation may be in order. In the meantime, a realistic survey of those motives presently in the ascendant offer a rich pageant of human diversity, that most intriguing of all marvels and wonders.

CHAPTER 2

MOTIVES DETERMINE DIRECTIONS

SUPERSTITION   HERO WORSHIP

PERFECTIONISTS   SENTIMENTALISTS

AVANT-GARDE   POST-GARDE

PATRIOTISM   NOSTALGIA   ''CAMPY''

TRIBUTE AND TROPHY   OSTENTATION

SOCIAL STATUS   PUBLIC IMAGE

OCCUPATION   FUNCTIONAL   FAMILY

TECHNICAL   TRAVEL   DIVERSION

CREATIVE   KOOKY   THERAPY

PERSONAL GROWTH   BEAUTY LOVER

SOMEONE ONCE SAID that every collection is a public confession, and certainly it expresses much about the personality of the creator, although not always in the most obvious manner. Tempting as it may be to consider analyzing character by means of the collection, it is more useful for the potential collector to note the variety of personal motivations that prompt the formation of collections.

Few will see themselves fitting exactly into the mold of a specific characterization, yet by objectively viewing, rather than by judging that whole battery of conscious and unconscious drives, the neophyte may find guidance and direction, or at least appreciate the need to examine individual incentives.

Having become convinced of the advantages, and attracted to the adventure of forming a collection, the best approach is to "collect" oneself and examine one's nature and life style. These, together with chance and circumstance, initiate imperceptible movements, until the incipient collector and the suitable opportunity come together. This is less destiny than destination.

❮ SUPERSTITION

Belief in the magical efficacy of an object, design, or material tends to make the believer accumulate more, in order to feel more fortunate and even safer from harm. Collections of objects thought to have some potency for bringing good or averting evil, such as elephants, owls, horseshoes, rabbits' feet, four-leaf clovers, and signs of the zodiac, are almost commonplace, requiring no inordinate superstition as an impetus, merely expressing a widespread primitive impulse.

Many collections consist entirely of personal talismans. Bees, turtles, swans, and butterflies are among figures chosen by individuals as their private lucky totem. Others prefer charms originating in individual cultures, such as scarabs of the Near East or the Sicilian hand to avert the evil eye.

Mr. Foot will collect shoes in all shapes, Mrs. Leaf acquires leaves in great variety, and the fox in every form attracts many

Foxes. Collections arrived at by reason of superstitious attachment may be trivial or tremendous; the truly lucky collector will trouble to make a worthwhile collection in any field.

(HERO WORSHIP

Whether it is unquestioning hero worship or merely a sympathetic response to a famous figure, people who are capable of intense dedication to some personality will often form collections of the possessions and memorabilia connected with that personality. Strangely, great artists may venerate colleagues considered their inferiors, and collect their works. Nothing is more personal than this accolade.

Napoleon, Lincoln, and Mozart are prime examples of adulation leading to great collections. In these cases it would seem that their greatness, although an outgrowth of their deeds, transcends them. The handkerchief and shoe buckle are collected as well as the important autograph. In classical times, the personality cult for Alexander the Great prompted Hannibal to pursue a bronze statuette by Lysippus that had belonged to the great Greek. On Hannibal's death it passed to the King of Bitthynia, from whom it was seized by Sulla and brought to Rome. Any object associated with Alexander in his lifetime would bring a fortune and was fought over by the powerful and mighty for centuries thereafter.

Although Churchill was a competent artist and Eisenhower an amateur, their paintings have brought high prices, based on their places in military and political rather than art history, and by personality rather than artistic considerations.

Not all hero worshipers stay with one hero; they form collections of autographs of record-holding baseball players, of gloves that belonged to famous actresses, or silk hats used by famous magicians.

It is a long way from the collector who prized the wine cup of Agamemnon to the groupie who treasures the beer can discarded by a rock singer; the hero-worshiping collector will have to find a place somewhere in between.

⟨ PERFECTIONISTS

Perfectionists become first-rate, if somewhat unhappy collectors. First-rate, because having set a goal, they are unceasing and unsparing in efforts to fulfill it. Unhappy, because they are never satisfied with what they achieve.

Condition being one of the principal problems for collectors in any field, perfectionists tend to choose subjects where broken, torn, split, ragged, or otherwise marred specimens are typically few. However, they will struggle, strain, and suffer to find examples as close to mint as possible, no matter what the specialty. This is usually a costly endeavor, so it is not unusual to find that perfectionists have small, if choice collections.

Yet it is said that perfectionists are among the leading collectors of coin and stamp errors, both growing specialties. Having eluded the eyes of inspectors, these "mistakes," which may be misstruck, misprinted, or mishandled by machines, have become costly prizes and achieved the ultimate proof of status; fake errors are becoming a major problem to collectors!

⟨ SENTIMENTALISTS

Romantic and sentimental types make natural collectors; although tying love letters with blue ribbon went out with gaslight, they prefer that to more mundane systems of filing. Emotional response will often start them collecting souvenirs such as valentines, ticket stubs, programs, perfume bottles, bouquet holders, and especially memorabilia connected with personal experience.

Sentimentalists tend to disorganized accumulations, whether or not neatly kept; tidiness may only simulate the sort of order required for a collection that needs to be internally structured. However, romantic material makes splendid collections when properly composed according to a plan. Victorian dance programs, French painted fans, sentimental sheet music, lace handkerchiefs, bonbon boxes, and love-knot jewelry are some of the older classics. Contemporary sentimentalists may collect these, but not surprisingly are finding less current material with which to launch romantic collections.

However, the seeds of great collections to come may yet germinate as sentimentally as some of the past. According to Charles Knoedler, the starting point of the Frick collection, one of the world's finest of masterpiece paintings, originated with a Bouguereau portrait of a little girl, bought because it resembled a daughter Henry Clay Frick had recently lost.

⟮ AVANT-GARDE

The need to be first with the last word motivates some sophisticates who see themselves as fashion leaders in collecting. Their choices may seem outrageous, ridiculous, amusing, or original, but are often cannily selected with an eye to profit. Just as fashion designers allow prominent people to wear their clothes at low or no cost, in return for publicizing them, so art dealers arrange with such figures to promote artists, movements, and trends by "collecting," giving parties where they are seen by others and mentioned by publicists.

On a more provincial level, a collector-hostess agrees to invite her friends to a "party" where a salesperson entertains them with "a collection" of limited-edition porcelain figures that just happen to be available for sale in lieu of kitchen pots.

Truly avant-garde collectors are usually in tune with the times, and fasten on something that is ripening but not quite ready to interest many. Art Deco, railroadiana, vintage movies, rock 'n' roll records, and American Indian pawn jewelry were collected by a handful of pioneers for several years before becoming immensely popular.

Some avant-gardists are alert for revival material, items that were once popularly collected but faded from the scene as trends changed. This was the case with oriental rugs, tapestries, and furniture made of animal horns.

❲ POST-GARDE

In contrast to the bold avant-garde spirits, some personalities are prone to conservation of tradition; for them collecting seems to flourish along well-beaten paths. Early American iron hinges, English pewter, Sheraton furniture, ancient coins, Ch'ien Lung porcelain, animalier bronzes, according to taste and purse, such staples prove most congenial to those with a strong taste for traditional values.

However, the fact that the subject of the collection is conventional does not mean that the viewpoint or its exposition in the actual formation is repetitive or dull. Original ideas and brilliant expression of them permit the guardian of the past a full rein of creativity in theme and viewpoint.

An outstanding example of this for the private collector was an exhibition at the Cloisters, New York City's bastion of the medieval. Illustrating life and art at the end of the Middle Ages, it included a wooden comb, brass level, cooking recipes, medical prescriptions, coins, Tudor knitwear, a farmer's manual for planting, and a pewter lavabo, among the several hundred items that vividly "explained" the past in a contemporary show-and-tell form.

❲ PATRIOTISM

Not necessarily a last refuge for collectors, patriotism does inspire collecting, and not only of documents and memorabilia, but also of characteristic national arts and crafts.

Judge Alphonse T. Clearwater made such a collection, which he presented to the Metropolitan Museum of·Art. Described as a "gracious, humorous, old-fashioned American," the judge, in his words, formed his collection of over five hundred pieces of American silver so that future generations would see "There existed in the American colonies and early in the States of the Republic . . . not only a refined taste creating a demand for beautiful silver, but an artistic instinct and skill upon the part of American silversmiths, enabling them to design and make articles of church and domestic silver, which in beauty of line and workmanship, well compares with the work of foreign silversmiths."

Not always so elegantly phrased or richly implemented, this respect, admiration, and pride in the work of forefathers motivate collections of folk, ethnic, and fine art throughout the world. Even in the U.S.S.R., where regional nationalism is not always encouraged, private collections expressing it continue to be assembled, defining an urge while defying restrictions.

Surges in national wealth have in recent times been accompanied by a rise in collections of national treasures by governments and private individuals. World markets are combed for a return of indigenous works. Japanese collectors dominated galleries and auctions for a period, until petrodollars displaced the yen as a magnet for the dealers and traders in antiques, art, and collectibles. Islamic treasures began to return to the Far East as a new galaxy of native collectors revived interest in their national heritage.

(NOSTALGIA

Often confused with sentiment, nostalgia is actually a longing to return to one's origins. Transposed into collecting, it becomes a desire to possess objects reminiscent of one's youth.

Personalities with a strong sense of nostalgia may, like Proust, find that some taste, odor, sound, or sight arouses deep springs of memory. However, instead of launching a novel, it might be the prelude for a collection. For the middle-aged and those nostalgic for times far different from these, such collecting is a happy transference from present reality. Collections of eighth-grade graduation cards, button hooks, pocket watches, napkin rings, wicker porch furniture, and even Sunday school medals offer pleasant and comparatively low-cost flights from the present.

A wave of nostalgic collecting by comparatively young people has created a new field, and incidentally a big business in ten- and twenty-year-old toys, puzzles, games, and comic books. Little Orphan Annie, Shirley Temple, and Howdy Doody, when in mint condition, like Cracker Jack puzzles, bring ransom-high prices from nostalgia-ridden collectors.

⟦ "CAMPY"

One generation's elegance may be another's "camp" or *kitsch*, exemplifying tastelessness. This satisfies some sense of the ridiculous and encourages the formation of collections combining an outlook of satire with that of humor. Often started in a joking spirit, they may continue in a more serious vein to express an important viewpoint about an era or style.

For those gifted with a sense of fun, or an ironical cast of mind, collecting offers a more constructive, if not creative, expression than playing practical jokes or making sharp comments, especially if employed to form original and amusing collections.

Some such collections are fairly predictable, consisting of comic valentines, complicated gadgets, racy bootjacks, trendy toys, lavatory signs, or cartoons. Others, more subtly based on social contrasts or changing values, include collections of Edwardian and Victorian clothing, furnishings, and trivia. Capturing the character of a former period that strikes us as amusing in terms of our own, they remind us that we shall not be spared when future generations laughingly collect what we consider smart.

⟦ TRIBUTE AND TROPHY

Not the least of the forces determining directions in collecting is rooted in the age-old reward of victory, namely loot. By biblical times, treasures and valuables were conventional trophies. Greek temples were pillaged by Romans to form their splendid collections of sculpture. World War II saw looting on greater scale than ever before, as the Nazis' Teutonic sense of order left little spared from their sweep.

However, on a more personal and peaceable level, also since time immemorial, the idea that "diamonds are a girl's best friend," a form of tribute and trophy to love, has inspired collections of antiques, art, and bibelots as well as jewelry. Madame de Verrue, a beautiful Parisian of the time of Louis XIV, preferred that her lovers show their appreciation by adding to her collection of Watteau, Lancret, Boucher, and Chardin paintings, as well as by gifts of furniture and objects of art, guiding their choice to the rarest and finest. At her death, when her famous collection was dispersed by sale, it was memorialized in a popular verse of the day:

> Here lies in a peace profound
> This lady of luxury
> Who, for certain security,
> Made her paradise on this round.

Also in an old tradition, diplomats, military figures, and heads of state are among those whose opportunities include forming interesting collections of value by reason of ceremonial gifts. United States law forbids federal employees to keep for their own use foreign gifts of more than minimal value, defined as fifty dollars. Such gifts become federal property.

During the Nixon scandals, a startled United States citizenry discovered that diamonds, jewels, antiques, rare weapons, silver, carpets, paintings, and objects of art were among the items that had been accepted by both elected politicians and other officials, some of whom had conveniently forgotten to officially record them, hence had not turned them over to the government. The procedure established with such gifts requires that they be sent to the State Department, which after disposing suitable material to government museums, places the balance on the auction block, putting the cash into the public coffers.

⟨ OSTENTATION

"I don't care what you call it, I just want my best friends to drop dead when they see it" is a sentiment that, though seldom spoken aloud, has spurred the formation of many overwhelming, showy, and occasionally excellent collections.

Those who live in opulent style tend to collect in a grand manner, forming collections of suitable treasures. Since the Shah of Iran considers it a requisite of hospitality to present a suitably elaborate table, his purchase for $129,000 of three hundred gold-decorated plates formerly in the collection of the royal Prussian court was considered a merely appropriate domestic addition.

A wave of flashy nineteenth-century European furniture and

works of art swept into the Near East on the wave of oil profits. Nineteenth-century Viennese, ormolu, and enamel-mounted cabinets, ornate Victorian silver, and new, expensive-looking silk carpets brought higher prices at London auctions than authentic eighteenth-century antiques from buyers eager to form "drop dead" collections.

Not all who prefer "show-off" material are wealthy. "Hand-painted" china and marcasite jewelry fulfill collecting standards of opulence and ostentation for some.

(SOCIAL STATUS

Absolutely nothing will expedite entrance into establishment society as readily as formation of a celebrated collection. Although in the latter twentieth century, little nobility or aristocracy remains to derogate new money, and old money seldom has the energy to point out parvenus, the qualifications still rule out "nobodies." But without other distinctions, "important" collectors will receive invitations to openings, memberships will be offered on benefit committees, and in general social acceptance by the "beautiful people" will follow for those who want it.

A collection is also something of a passport into less glamorous circles and more than once has provided contacts into segments of suburbia that might otherwise offer no entering wedge. The aura of social esteem that surrounds collectors is a vestige of former times, but it carries over because there still is a mystique about discrimination and superior taste as reflecting a high level of culture.

On any level, the role of status in collecting can only serve as a questionable impetus. Yet whatever the origin, it may launch an outstanding collection. People may start to collect impelled by a need for status, but they usually go on to form collections because they have become involved in a satisfying project.

(PUBLIC IMAGE

Even before professionals became fixtures on the public-relations scene, tycoons were aware of the importance of establishing a life style that reflected credit (often literally) on them and their enterprises. The general public is aware that public-relations experts project images of their clients, but it does not always recognize that the role of collector has been employed for that purpose in the past as well as the present.

Dealers such as Duveen built their own financial empires about the turn of the twentieth century by teaching men of limited education and background, who had risen to positions of great wealth and were facing the public as heads of large business enterprises, that forming a collection was a path to public esteem as well as private status.

To be very rich without forming a collection is often to lack a positive image, and huge corporations such as IBM, U. S. Steel, Chase Manhattan Bank, and First National Bank of Chicago have been drawn into collecting to reinforce an acceptable profile. An official of one such company believes that its art collection "predisposes some customers to do business with us"; another notes, "the art collection denotes a high-quality company." The corporate collector is a new factor on the collecting scene.

One corporate bank expeditiously trades its collection, buying and selling to show a profit, possibly mollifying stockholders who might prefer dividends to art. Important executives are said to enjoy playing the role of Maecenas to living artists, and some have been known to make advantageous purchases for their private collections as a result of business contacts.

(OCCUPATION

A popular pianist whose preference for piano-shaped swimming pools extends to a limitless variety of piano-shaped objects has achieved several decades of valuable publicity for this collection, but countless thousands of musicians and music lovers collect items incorporating musical themes without fanfare, but simply because forming such a collection satisfies a sense of identity and strengthens the bonds of association.

Similarly, physicians form collections of antique medical instruments; wine merchants collect drinking paraphernalia; opticians hunt antique spectacles; locksmiths search for antique locks and keys, and fashion designers for period clothing.

Gifted stage designer Donald Oenslager followed the bent of his career to collect scenic sketches of stage settings. These included original baroque and rococo inventions as well as nineteenth- and twentieth-century drawings to illustrate the development of stage design. Exhibited, the collection evoked compliments from critics for its contribution to artistic as well as dramatic history.

Some are indirectly "called" to collecting by their calling. A profession, business, or trade with which the individual is involved may provide the impetus as well as the subject.

Browsing in a bookshop, Kenneth Lang, a Doubleday publishing executive, came across a first edition of one of his firm's earliest publications. It impelled him to start a collection with the purpose of gathering the complete list up to 1910. When Robert Mangieri, a young insurance man, discovered that signed letters from some of his important clients were valuable, he was on his way to an autograph collection. In some cases, occupation is opportunity as well as incentive.

Edward H. Mosler, Jr., head of a safe manufacturing firm, became a leading collector of mechanical banks, and in addition formed a collection of forgeries and cast-iron toys rigged to imitate the real thing.

Frank Tallman, a great flier and stuntsman, collected World War I planes and flew his antiques for pleasure and profit in appropriate movies.

The first great American autograph collector, Dr. William B. Sprague (1795–1876), got his start accumulating historical signatures when he served as tutor to George Washington's grandnephew, who provided authentic source material.

⟨ FUNCTIONAL

Many a fine collection has started with the functional incentive of furnishing a household. Most of the great furniture collections originated with the utilitarian motive of supplying comfortable furnishings suitable to the style of the house and its inhabitants' manner of life. The Jones and Wallace collections, Britain's most splendid illustrations of French eighteenth-century domestic furniture and accessories, were personal backgrounds for both their ambitious collectors.

Period country dwellings that need to be furnished will often induce their owners to do so in the original style, and when old residential districts in cities such as Savannah, Georgia, and Charleston, South Carolina, are restored, numerous collectors are encouraged to give their interiors authenticity.

While decorating a home with period antiques does not necessarily lead to forming a collection, it often blazes a trail toward a specific direction, and Early American, Federal American, and Victorian households serve as most acceptable framework for outstanding collections, throughout the United States.

([FAMILY

With the rise of the middle class in Europe and the United States in the nineteenth century came a great desire on its part to simulate the roots that nourished the landed gentry it was displacing. "Family portraits" that were bought rather than inherited were a first step, and thereafter family crests on silver, china, and even linen followed to imply high-born lineage, often ridiculed in both literature and life as pretentious snobbery.

However, although the importance of the family has receded, it has not altogether disappeared; an entire industry is based on family crest research, which still employs thousands working in archives in London alone. In addition, a London dealer specializes in British armorial crests, buying up what he finds interesting, and after tracing contemporary descendants, he offers them the opportunity to acquire the crested treasure as the start of a collection.

Inherited family possessions can become the nucleus of all sorts of collections. Campaign buttons found in his grandfather's desk started one collector on a lifetime project. A young woman's discovery of family photographs taken over the past hundred years impelled her to form a collection which, when exhibited, drew great praise as a biographical essay of exceptional originality.

❨ TECHNICAL

Clock repairmen become clock collectors and, contrariwise, clock collectors become skillful at clock repairs, a compensation that balances out well for expertise in this popular field, encouraging the formation of collections.

A television repairman in California found some old radio sets in a shop he bought, and finding time on his hands to repair them, went on to form an outstanding and nationally admired collection of vintage radios.

Appreciation of the skills that go into making, designing, and keeping things going, combine to form seedbeds for collecting. The ability to perceive minute and subtle differences of craft and design, and also to be in command of the techniques for restoration, gives an individual obvious incentives; add to this occasions for making purchases at attractive "inside" prices and a good line on unusual sources for parts.

Originally a gunsmith, collector George Herron, first made himself a knife because he couldn't find one that suited him. When it was seen by a knife enthusiast who persuaded the maker to sell it to him for his collection, it started a demand that eventually made the South Carolina gunsmith into a knifemaker and a knife collector as well. Since other collectors entreat him to accept their orders for his knives and willingly queue for examples of his craft, he is in a good position to trade to form his own collection.

❨ TRAVEL

Life style incorporating travel, even though it may be based on comparatively short vacations rather than extended grand tours, encourages collections. The young couple on vacation in Canada, noting an exhibition and sale of Eskimo sculpture, who acquire a piece and with it an interest and awareness, have made the first step leading to the formation of a collection. In the late nineteenth century, Mrs. John Crosby Brown, while strolling in Florence, heard a flute played, stimulating her interest in antique instruments. That flute became the nucleus of a collection of hundreds of extraordinary pieces, which she later presented to the Metropolitan Museum of Art and which is world famous.

Incentive to buy is not always incentive to collect; attics and cellars are full of random purchases made abroad. Yet when these are weeded and culled, later generations may well find them to be springboards for their burgeoning collections.

The collector on a holiday trip is never your shepherded tourist, requiring entertainment. To be a collector is to have a purpose, and to fulfill the opportunity gives wings to tennis sneakers, wooden clogs, or neatly tied oxfords.

([DIVERSION

"A new concept that combines dinner, live showcase entertainment, and the thrills of the Auction . . . of course the wine is on the house," reads a metropolitan newspaper advertisement. "Backroads touring, weekend bus trips to out-of-the-way antique shops and fleamarkets" also appears in newspapers' entertainment pages, tempting collectors out of the city. Collecting has always been a diverting activity; now it has become a diversion, a form of showmanship and amusement.

The ultimate diversion, forming a collection, is also gaining in popularity, partly as an outgrowth of random collecting, but largely because those who have become even slightly involved find that they become deeply absorbed. Rather than serving as mere entertainment or pastime, collecting relieves tension and pressure because it centers attention on a living, organic arrangement, diverting to, rather than from, and thus adding a positive interest.

([CREATIVE

Although the much-touted joys of browsing and buying are real enough and not to be underestimated in appraising the satisfactions of collecting, too often the chief delight, that of creativity, is overlooked.

As every artist—whether sculptor, painter, weaver, photog-

rapher, or writer—selects subject and viewpoint, so does the collector. Many who have other creative gifts enjoy collecting as well,
but for some with no special talent in the arts or crafts, collecting
becomes the creative outlet with which they fulfill their need to
comment on the world as it was, is, should, or might be.

"I had always wanted to do something, write a book, or invent
a machine," said George Costakis, the Moscow art collector whose
private collection, admired internationally, has given him something "to do" that is distinguished and creative indeed. Art historians, critics, and collectors make special trips to Moscow to see
this outstanding collection of Russian futurist painting and sculpture which he constantly enriches by searching out hitherto unknown works. Creatively collecting against the tide of establishment taste, he has no competition from Russian museums.

(KOOKY

Collecting is so widely accepted as a form of neurosis that it is a
commonplace for collectors to call themselves "nutty." Those
who collect Faberge's Easter eggs made for the Czar, and those
who pursue the paper and cardboard variety will jokingly share
self-imposed claims to slight touches of aberration.

Actually, collectors not only enjoy the same degree of mental
health as the general population, but it has also been noted that
collecting alleviates more neuroses than it causes, although exas-
perated relatives and even dealers will sometimes question that.
As a rule, when as is sometimes said, collecting has taken someone
"round the bend," it is more likely that the individual has made
the turn, taking the collection along.

Collecting gone wild goes well beyond the borders of eccen-
tricity; it is expressed in hoarding unlikely items without selection
or classification, and without a logical or reasonable theme or end
in view. Kleptomania is a true aberration and has traditionally
affected collectors. The custom of dealers to rush the bill to the
house before the magpie collector arrived home has probably
disappeared; it was not uncommon when most collectors were
affluent and dealers knew where they lived and how to reach
them.

([THERAPY

Forming a collection serves a simple therapeutic function for some, permitting dreams and fantasies to be expressed in a constructive framework of planned acquisition. It may be the result of frustration. The woman who can't travel, can collect teacups from every country she would like to visit. The unfulfilled archaeologist can form a collection of pre-Columbian figures. Many a man who as a boy dreamed of becoming a big-league pitcher collects old baseball cigarette and gum cards and feels less cut off from youthful hopes.

More complicated neuroses, better known to the analyst's notebook, are as varied as individual obsessions. Fetishists have masked their more or less perverse fascinations, and doubtless done no one harm in their collectors' roles. Without this outlet, the dark pages of crime and mental disorder might record a greater volume than they do. Psychoanalyst Erich Fromm says in *Anatomy of Human Destructiveness*, "If man cannot create anything or make a dent in anything . . . he can escape the unbearable sense of powerlessness and nothingness only by affirming himself in the act of destruction of the life that he is unable to create."

Forming a collection may be a form of sublimation; if so, it has much to recommend it as an escape that is entirely absorbing, and by selectively bringing related objects into meaningful and unified entity, helps the individual feel successful in overcoming the inevitable destruction of the life force.

([PERSONAL GROWTH

Often achieved by travail and tempering on the anvil of life's difficulties, personal growth can also be advanced with less distress and more pleasure in the process of creating a collection. The forethought required for long-term planning, the need for objective analysis, the discipline of self-imposed goals, and the satisfactions deferred are sources of development and enrichment.

More than one kind of judgment is tested in the formation of a collection. Decisions are made as to the quality of people as well as of things, and collecting becomes a microcosm of life.

Although collectors can be observed objectively by outsiders, fellow collectors combine insight with perspective. Even generous souls have moments of covetousness; the most honest might consider a sneaky ploy; and the meanest rise to moments of compassion for a colleague caught in the web of unfortunate circumstance. Not infallibly, but in many cases, to form a collection enlarges the spirit and promotes tolerance.

⟮ BEAUTY LOVER

It is too often taken for granted that those with a great love for beauty will make outstanding collectors. Not always so. Bernard Berenson, critic and scholar, who helped others make some of the greatest collections of Renaissance art, did have some handsome and interesting paintings and art objects in his villa, but above all, he "collected" the glorious Tuscan sunsets he watched almost every evening of his life. Others, less aesthetically sensitive, formed famous and valuable collections with his counsel.

On the whole, however, the individual who will buy flowers before bread does tend to be a collector who will not see objects as mere things, but as having inherent qualities to be admired and cherished. That's a good start.

Some find beauty in fine art, others in what may seem to be mundane, even common artifacts. The important aspect of forming any collection is not the collector's vision of beauty, but the intelligence and viewpoint focused on any subject undertaken.

CHAPTER 3

THE COMMITMENT

(CONSIDER THE SUBSTANCE *pottery* *porcelain* *glass* *brass* *bronze* *copper* *iron and steel* *pewter* *tin* *gold* *silver* *ivory and bone* *leather and hair* *paper* *shell* *stone* *synthetics* *textiles* *wood*

(CONSIDER THE PURPOSE

(CONSIDER THE MAKER

(WHERE WAS IT MADE?

(HOW WAS IT MADE?

(TO WHOM DID IT BELONG?

(WHEN WAS IT MADE?   (HOW BIG IS IT?

(COLOR FACTORS   (STYLE

(SUBJECT MATTER

(THEME AND VIEWPOINT

UNDERSTANDABLY OVERWHELMED, if not bewildered by the range of choice, it may seem to beginning collectors that all the possibilities float in some enormous, amorphous grab bag into which the collector extends a hand, hoping chance will press a prize into groping fingers.

Actually, while the scope is encyclopedic, it is neither incomprehensible nor chaotic. Arranged under simple and logical classifications, cross-indexed for advantages and personal preferences, and co-ordinated with the principles that transcend subject, there is an almost automatic conversion on theme and viewpoint. Thus the selection is narrowed to a commitment that has relevance to the individual's personality and purpose.

⟨ CONSIDER THE SUBSTANCE

To separate the appeal of the material itself from the way it is wrought—when, where, and by whom—is difficult if not impossible, yet many collect glass, pottery, porcelain, copper, brass, or pewter because they respond to the substance itself.

The individual qualities of wood, iron, paper, or tin control not only the techniques by which they are crafted, but also the forms into which they can be made; yet for those who collect by material, this triangle is dominated by the former, and they structure their collections accordingly.

The distinction takes on somewhat different emphasis in considering intrinsically valuable substances such as gold, silver, ivory, and precious and semiprecious stones, but here also the value-free appeal of the material for its own sake must be taken into consideration if the standards for creative collecting are to be met. Those who lust for gold only because it is precious rarely create great collections of gold objects, but those who lust for pewter are likely to form outstanding collections in that medium.

POTTERY

Playing with mud, our ancestors made the first pottery. It appears early in every culture as hand-patted, sun-dried, unglazed clay objects, and goes on to be glazed, turned on the wheel, and variously decorated. Early specimens are highly prized for their craft and artistic expression.

Certain periods in history have produced outstanding pottery, and ancient Greece, China, and Etruria are among the classic examples. Later types—Hispano-Mooresque from Spain and North Africa, Majolica from Italy, Faience from France, and Holland's Delft—intrigue collectors, and it seems that every country has its heritage of pottery, whether as folk art or sophisticated craft, sometimes both.

North American Indian, Mexican, and other Latin American pre-Columbian and later examples of pottery are admired and collected and often serve as inspiration for contemporary pottery, also the focus for collections.

Some collectors are interested in both antique and modern pottery, but most specialize. American pottery of the Colonial period is rare and eagerly sought. Britain exported much, then and later in the nineteenth century, even after many American factories were founded, sending forth huge quantities for growing mass markets. The trend to collecting pottery of American factories has brought names such as Rookwood, Van Briggle, Newcomb, and Roseville to the forefront, and followers of Art Nouveau and Art Deco design find much to collect in twentieth-century pottery.

PORCELAIN

Searching for greater hardness than pottery afforded, the Chinese had developed stoneware, a harder, denser material that some collect as Wedgwood Jasperware and some as German steins or American pickle crocks.

By the ninth century, the Chinese had discovered that petuntse, a feldspar stone, would mix with fine white clay at very high heat to produce true, hard-paste porcelain. This was cherished, admired, and collected from the beginning by Chinese and by Europeans who imported it, and who tried to copy it.

At first European efforts brought forth those soft-paste porcelains, a mixture of clay with glass "frit," now treasures of great rarity and price, discouraging all but the wealthiest collectors. Eventually, the secret of true hard-paste porcelain was "discovered" in

Saxony, Germany, and from the time the first factory was founded at Meissen in 1710, collectors have sought and formed collections of fine porcelain objects.

Some factories have been in existence for hundreds of years; new ones come and go. Identifying marks for both pottery and porcelain may tell the name of the factory, the name of the manager, the artist modeler, the decorator, the name of the town, a series date, the trademark of the owner, the name of the potter, or that of the retailer.

GLASS

Probably because its fragility defies as it courts disaster, glass is said to appeal to the greatest number of collectors. It is the permanent bubble that may break, but can never really burst.

Availability of fire, the raw materials consisting of sand and alkali, and the simple tools required, combined to produce the type we still know as soda glass or "green" glass. This is unbleached and naturally colored without art and may be coiled, blown, or molded.

The Egyptians introduced chemicals to make specifically colored glass, and by Roman imperial times, some of the most valuable collections consisted of the multicolored murrhine. In the early sixteenth century, Venetians clarified clear glass, calling it "crystal," and also enriched the color spectrum, principally with ruby, which they got by using chloride of gold.

In England in 1674, a man by the name of Ravenscroft replaced the alkalines hitherto used with oxide of lead, giving us what was then called "flint" glass and what we term lead crystal.

Although marks are often lacking, names of makers and sources of glass structure many collections, especially in the art glass field, where they can be more readily traced. Pattern determines the outline of collections of pattern and cut glass; technique, form and color in the Early American field.

Following the boom in Carnival and Depression glass, both mass-produced, interest has been built to develop collectors' interests in such glass factories as Heisey and Imperial, in which the emphasis seems to be on assortments and rarities.

BRASS

This metal can represent the homely domestic virtues or the heights of artistry. It has been known as poor man's gold, yet was used for the most precious reliquaries in the twelfth century. Paul Revere made brass as well as silver objects, as did many silversmiths. Glowing, malleable, but not necessarily soft, brass is made from a mixture of copper and zinc; weight and design determine resistance to wear, and the end product can be tawdry or splendid.

In the Victorian period, brass poured forth from a seemingly limitless cornucopia of production, handcrafted, or industrially and mass-produced, the latter two not necessarily interchangeable. To economize on metal, one device was made to explode a fine sheet of brass into a mold, resulting in hollow, thin, but attractive doorknobs and finials. Scales, mortars, trivets, jugs, student lamps, sconces, and bedsteads were among the many objects made in fine-quality, heavy, or solid brass, as well as cheap commercial, often brass-plated examples.

BRONZE

Its very weight, even in small objects, assumes there will be a serious approach to a collection of bronzes. While it is not uncommon to hear collectors say that they collect glass, brass, pottery, or ivory, one rarely hears "I collect bronze." In addition to being heavy, it is very strong, and it is this quality that brought man to a new stage of development in the Bronze Age, when the material, possibly the first man-made alloy, resulted from a mixture of copper and tin.

Because bronze requires a special form of craftsmanship, the earliest weapons, tools, and ritual and domestic articles made in bronze seem to qualify as works of art in their own terms as well as ours. Dating as far back as 3000 B.C., Scythian, Luristan, Chinese, and Celtic examples are among the prized possessions of the greatest museums and outstanding private collections.

Greek, Roman, Byzantine, medieval, and Renaissance artists and artisans continued the bronze tradition, the latter on the highest level as the Baptistery bronze doors by Ghiberti testify.

Unfortunately, like other metals, bronze can be melted down and recast, so its inherent durability depends on circumstance, and while some survives, much is destroyed in every era. However, collectors are drawn to conserve it, and not only famous works of art in bronze, but also bronze lamps, inkwells, vases, bells, miniature figures, medals, plaques, and doorknockers are acquired to enrich newly formed collections in every generation.

Bronze is particularly valued by collectors for its patina, a coating resulting from oxidation and ranging in tone from pale gray to deep turquoise. Some collectors of bronze have been accused of collecting patina first and the item as an afterthought.

COPPER

Reminiscent of fire and the red rock from which it originated, the glow of copper appeals to collectors, possibly as it did to the nomadic tribesmen who found it accidentally over seven thousand years ago and painstakingly learned to master it. Except for gold, copper is believed to have been the first metal to stimulate and challenge man as an artisan. Tools, weapons, storage receptacles, cooking pots, and ornaments of copper were produced in early cultures.

Although it has been joined, and for many purposes superseded, by other metals since, it has retained a special place in the kitchen, where antique copper holds sway in the form of kettles, saucepans, pots, jugs, molds, and countless other utensils. Copper cooking vessels must be lined with tin, but are readily retinned, and deterioration of the lining is no deterrent to a collector who finds another otherwise sturdy piece.

Collectors who favor antique copper have a wide selection of attractive objects in this metal, including weathervanes, wine cisterns, measures, trays, boxes, and fireplace equipment. Contemporary craftspeople employ copper for ornament, both personal and domestic, and some collectors consider modern copper pieces as works of art.

IRON AND STEEL

Sturdy and earthy or elegant and refined, iron in every shape and form attracts collectors. Many of them seem to respond to it as a folk art form, while others prefer its fine art or sophisticated guise; but all refer to its tough and yet responsive characteristics.

Subject to rust and corrosion, ancient iron is not plentiful; little is found that can be dated to its beginnings about 2000 B.C. Beau-

tiful antique wrought iron, especially found in Spain and throughout Europe in churches and palaces as grilles, screens, and bal-
conies, requires careful maintenance. Small sections of larger units
are sought by collectors.

Specialists seek firebacks, fireplace equipment, locks, keys,
hinges, doorstops, doorknockers, cast-iron furniture, and stoves.

A combination of wrought and forged iron gave us steel, first
collected as blades by those who found it gave them a superb
weapon. However, jewelry of cut steel, and steel furniture are
among other forms that collectors appreciate.

PEWTER

Tough and long-wearing if kept away from direct heat, mostly tin
with copper and lead alloys, pewter has a sober, sensible austerity
that arouses great passion in collectors. Roman pewter has been
found in Britain, guilds of pewterers were formed in the late Middle Ages throughout Europe. Chinese pewter is often combined
decoratively with brass, to the benefit of both metals.

Remaining popular into the nineteenth century, pewter was
made in many qualities; for the most part, the best has remained
to form collections. Much of the rest was melted down as it became worn. A somewhat debased form of pewter called Britannia
metal at one time replaced pewter in popularity; Britannia metal
too has become a popular collectible.

Almost any practicably copied item made in silver has also appeared in pewter, with the addition of utilitarian every-day objects, especially suited to the cottage kitchen and tavern. Touch
marks identify, but some of the best pieces have no marks at all.

Pewter collectors have increasingly found themselves paying
prices for fine antique pieces that rival those asked for similar
items less rare in their silver equivalents. Fine American pewter attracts an increasing number of collectors as its scarcity grows. In-
depth study presents problems of attribution that are especially
challenging and produce an ever higher level of scholarship on the
part of pewter collectors.

TIN

Tin fanciers arrange themselves in several ranks. One group con-
sists of specialists in painted or plain antique folk examples; a sec-

ond, of those who prefer antique European and oriental tole, with its finely detailed and embellished scenes and designs. A third category of collectors is interested in the more commercial forms of the nineteenth and early twentieth centuries, while a fourth collects more recently made tin containers in an area now known as "advertising tin."

Folk tin includes lanterns, buckets, and basins—in general as utilitarian country wares. Elegant tole appears in umbrella stands, tea and coffee urns, sconces, vases, shelves, and cachepots. Commercial tin, antique or vintage, will include food containers for the most part, tea and coffee boxes, and spice boxes and biscuit tins stenciled, lithographed, or transfer printed.

GOLD

The effulgent allure of gold is well based on its virtues as a metal; it was used for objects of luxury before it became a medium of exchange. While packing much value into small bulk, and almost indestructible, it can be wrought into objects of great beauty.

In its pure state of 24 karats, it serves as bullion but is too soft for other purposes; hence it is alloyed at standards of 22, 18, 14, 12, and even lower karat proportions. This is always a factor of concern when it cannot be exactly assayed due to absence of technical skill or unwillingness to pay for the cost of assay.

Gold is said to be the first metal used by man in its natural combination with silver, a material the ancients called electrum.

Some collect gold-plated, gold-washed, gold-filled and rolled gold objects; pinchbeck gold, a gilded alloy of brass named for its eighteenth-century inventor, has many adherents and admirers among collectors. However, high quality gold objects, whether in decorative and sculptural forms or as eating and drinking vessels, flatware, rare coins and medals, ritual or religious objects, snuffboxes, toilet articles, as paraphernalia to express the panoply of power, or as jewelry to bedeck and beautify, have been collected for many thousands of years, more often as a form of wealth and security than for the merit of the piece apart from its material. At the same time there are collectors who acquire African gold weights, hand-wrought vessels, or pieces of fine jewelry for their meaning in terms of craft or other value virtues besides the metal. The exhibition in the United States of the millennia-old Scythian gold treasure from Russian and other museums testified to the splendid uses to which artisans have always put a splendid material.

SILVER

You rarely hear a silver collector contradict the person who proclaims that "nobody wants silver anymore, it's too difficult to keep it polished." Silver collectors *love* to polish their treasures, but on the whole, they'd prefer to have less competition in the marketplace and are quite happy to discourage it.

The empathy for silver overrides so-called practicality, and is based on an appreciation for this marvelous metal with its inherent response to the craftsman's artistry.

Silver is second to gold in value, but because silver is more available, it is much more generally collected. Pure silver, unalloyed, has been used for making objects, but is too soft to stand much wear. It is best alloyed with copper, and the English standard, known as *sterling*, .925 pure silver, is the most renowned and has been since the fourteenth century in Britain, and for over a century in the United States.

Coin silver, .900 pure silver, was popular in the United States until about midnineteenth century, although sterling quality was also used by the best early silversmiths who followed the English example.

In England, *Sheffield silver*, a hydraulically pressed sandwich of two layers of sterling with a layer of copper between, served to economize on costly silver from 1740 until the 1840s, when electroplating became popular. Unappreciated by collectors at the beginning of this century, Sheffield silver has since become a treasured collectible.

Various types and qualities of silver plated over base metals were made throughout the Victorian era and continue to be made today. This includes silver electroplated on copper, incorrectly dubbed "Sheffield," albeit so stamped.

European silver, called "Continental" as a category, was produced over the centuries in various combinations of alloy; it is usually in the .800 range of purity.

Contemporary silvercraft is at a high level, and many collect hand-wrought pieces in all forms from hollow ware to jewelry.

IVORY AND BONE

Precisely, ivory is derived solely from the elephant's tusk, although the tusks of fossil mammoths, hippopotami, walruses, narwhals, and rhinoceros horns are similar substances, sometimes difficult to distinguish.

Ivory takes a highly polished finish and permits a delicate precision of detail, rare in other materials suitable for carving. It has been said that it would be possible to trace the history of taste from earliest times to the present entirely in carved ivories, so consistent has its hold been. The exotic source, its comparative rarity, and the artistry and craftsmanship lavished on it have combined to excite collectors for thousands of years.

From police parade batons, cane handles, fans, crucifixes and reliquaries, snuffboxes, portrait busts, and medallions to furniture and smaller objects inlaid with this material, ivory collecting covers a vast panorama.

Not as finely grained, although quite receptive to the skilled carver's tool, carved bone figures, combs, beads, plaques, and buttons vie with those in ivory and are often remarkably similar in appearance, although rarely in value.

LEATHER AND HAIR

Devotees of leather, whether as bookbinding, saddlery, furniture, medieval pilgrim flasks, or in that remarkable boule curie treatment that hardened and conserved the leather in a permanent mold, prefer to understate their enthusiasm, lest an already limited field be invaded. Actually, leather offers the collector a material that endures for hundreds of years if properly tanned and treated and compassionately handled.

Shagreen etuis, seal trunks, and Indian garments are among the items sought in a single issue of a generalist antiques publication. Fire buckets, helmets, flagons, and portmanteaus intrigue others, while gun holsters are subjects of classification as valid as any.

Everyone has heard of haircloth and horsehair fabric, but decorative pictures and mourning jewelry are a special taste. However, if appealing, all sorts of hair jewelry, and especially the elaborate creations of figures and objects that are glass-dome Victorian rarities, keep this specialist-collector in thrall.

PAPER

Some paper objects, like stamps and paper money, have value because of what has been printed on them; however, there are many other aspects of collectibility, as paper carpets patented in 1819, paper figures, and papier-mâché testify.

Invented in China about A.D. 100, next made in the Near East, brought to Spain by the Saracens in the twelfth century, whence the manufacture spread to the rest of Europe, much of paper's later use in the form of books and prints paralleled the development of printing.

Rice paper; rag paper; currency paper; embossed paper; foil, waxed, and oiled papers, and painted and printed wallpaper unrolls a list of only a few varieties and their variations. Paper dolls, games, toy theaters, toys, silhouettes, cut-work, umbrellas, fans, and playing cards are classic subjects of paper collecting. More recently, book jackets and record covers, invalid, outdated stock certificates, diplomas, Dixie cup lids, baseball and other sports cards, comic books, and magazines have been added.

Whether or not the twentieth century will go down in history as a "disposable" era depends on how many of its vast assortments of paper goods go into collections now being formed. It may also depend on how fast modern paper deteriorates—much of it is made with chemicals that cause it to self-destruct.

SHELL

"Sea shells from the seashore" in all their infinite variety capture the imagination today as they have for millennia, serving as currency, toys, jewelry, utensils, and domestic decoration, and at the same time as a testimony to the wonders of nature.

Whether scientific or aesthetic, shell collectors exercise all degrees of connoisseurship, and their collections reflect this in size and scope. Another variety of shell collector acquires not so much the specimen as the construction into which it has been organized. Thus boxes, mirror frames, napkin rings, and various types of bric-a-brac form separate categories of shell collecting. In addition, mother-of-pearl, used for buttons, fans, opera glasses, jewelry, and worked with papier-mâché into trays, boxes, and furniture, characterizes other aspects of shell collecting.

The carapace of the hawksbill tortoise, the hard covering of the armadillo, and the outside calcareous layer of bird's eggs also engage collectors. Translucent and attractively mottled tortoise shell is so popular it has contributed to the possible extinction of its bearer. Collectors of antique tortoise combs, toilet articles, boxes, fans, and furniture inlaid with this material may appreciate its rarity without further contributing to its future disappearance. However, when species are endangered, shells, like feathers and skins, may become off-limit commodities no matter what the vintage, subject to import and other government regulation.

STONE

An affinity for some kind of stone is as natural as the shape of the human hand that it accompanied on the ascent of mankind. Marble appeals to the sculptor because it can be mastered, and to the collector *because* it has been mastered. Children collect stones automatically as a form of play; adults collect them for display and, if intrinsically valuable as gems, as a form of security.

Precious stones, cut or uncut, share with silver and gold the standing of treasure, and history is full of deeds, largely criminal, for their acquisition.

Semiprecious stones become more precious with skillful carving, and from rock crystal to the variously colored varieties, they have been ardently collected for many centuries.

Jade has a special mystique in many cultures, but principally in China, where its craft has reached the highest artistry in awe for the durable that is beautiful and precious.

Fossils and natural mineral forms have become so popularly collected that fortunes have been made by dealers who have gone into this trade, and sophisticated collectors search out rarities with which market prices keep stride.

SYNTHETICS

Celluloid was produced commercially as early as 1868 and is considered the first of what has become an astounding array. Daguerreotype cases made of gutta-percha are not, strictly speaking, made of a synthetic material, but are considered by some to fit into the framework of such a collection. Many collections of these so-called antiques of the future are under way. One collection of plastics limits itself to those that simulate other materials; another includes decorative objects using plastic in some original and unusual fashion. The choice of collectibles is no longer restricted to animal, vegetable, and mineral!

Museums of modern art throughout the world have made it a practice to exhibit superior examples of outstanding or prize-winning objects in contemporary design in man-made materials, from kitchen ware to kites to sculpture. Aware collectors use these criteria as well as their own judgment in acquiring what they believe are the characteristic artifacts of our era that will take on importance and value when the collectors of the future appraise twentieth-century design and materials.

TEXTILES

Here again is a material to which some react with appreciation—people who collect uncommon examples do so with fervor born of knowledge and understanding.

Seemingly fragile, yet surprisingly durable, cotton, linen, silk, and wool, with sometimes threads of metal, feathers, and other unusual admixtures, have been preserved for thousands of years in fortuitous circumstances. A carpet over twenty-five hundred years old was found safeguarded by permafrost in a tomb in Russia, and sheer linen sealed in sun-baked Egyptian tombs has outlived empires.

Embroidery and other fine needlework, laces and quilts are among the prizes that collectors seek in ever greater numbers with the growth of appreciation for the old textiles and the contemporary handcraft developments as well.

Floor coverings, from precious antique oriental palace carpets to rag rugs made for cabins and farmhouses, have their place in collections that usually specialize in either the luxurious or folk variety, with both finding connoisseurs to acquire and appreciate them.

Clothing and costumes of the long-distant and more recent past have found growing favor with collectors. Garments and useful or purely decorative fabric furnishings of historic periods are not readily available, but those interested seek them out by tracing descendants, owner-collectors, contacting dealers, and following auctions. What may seem fortuitous finds are often the end result of persistently following a trail through documents and other means.

The clothing of Victorian times and earlier decades of this century are being worn as well as collected. Fine designer clothes, acquired by museums as well as private collections, and in some cases, certain items of common attire that were mass-produced, shown by the Smithsonian Institution, have given the stamp of acceptance to what some formerly considered old, secondhand clothes. Some of the garments, found in thrift shops, even give a certain social cachet to their self-declared wearer-collectors.

WOOD

Lovingly and sensuously palming an antique burl maple bowl, one collector of woodenware takes pleasure in grain and texture as evoked by skillful workmanship; others' directions may lead to African ritual objects, snuffboxes, miniature- or conventional-size furniture, or oriental Buddhas; the collector of wood can take many turnings.

Collections of wood objects can be formed to illustrate the variety of woods available, with emphasis on rarities such as zebra, palisander, holly, or sycamore in various combinations, often inlaid in fine antique furniture.

A Gothic linenfold panel, a Renaissance copy in wood of a small Roman bronze statuette, and modern wood abstract sculpture all fit into the collection of a devotee of this natural formation with its universal appeal.

Grass and reeds in the form of baskets, figures, and other objects, especially in folk and ethnic arts, inspire interesting collections of what is, after all, wood in the making.

⟮ CONSIDER THE PURPOSE

What is it for? Truffle slicers, inkwells, bells, bottles, teapots, scissors, knife rests, and watch fobs are among the myriad objects collected according to their function, as are countless other tools, utensils, ornaments, and instruments. Almost every object has a purpose; this can become the framework for almost any collection.

Some even collect archaic objects of unknown purpose, in order to discover what they were made to accomplish. In contrast, seemingly useless objects are collected by others because they take pleasure in the very absence of utility.

Collections with ambitious scope based on function can be overwhelming. Railroadiana, known by its buffs as "railroad mania," is such an example, and a few have been able to acquire a private full-size or narrow-gauge railroad, track on which to run it, and a station. However, most who want to collect some aspect of transportation by rail, settle for individual segments of the larger function. Timetables, railroad lanterns, station clocks, dining car equipment, station signs, uniforms, or even buttons are the narrower channels into which collectors are forced by necessity.

⟮ CONSIDER THE MAKER

Certain collections contain the work of one person, of a family, a single workshop, a school under a particular influence, even a factory. Indeed, to discover such a unified source and to form an integrated collection before others become aware of its desirability is the dream of most collectors.

Nor is it just for the magnetism of a name, since it is possible for creators to be anonymous, but because the body of the work qualifies as worthy of the structure of a collection. Shaker-made objects might have only the name of the sect for identification; few of its skilled artisans are individually known.

However, to fix on a maker in the limited or wider sense is to follow a path that may be strewn with obstacles, but nonetheless has the advantages of a direction and well-defined goal. Atwater Kent radios, William Morris decorations, Dorothy Doughty birds, Paul Storr silver, Currier & Ives prints, Lalique glass, and Faberge jewelry are subjects for maker-oriented collections, as are Waterman pens and Parker games.

It is not unusual for collectors of art to choose one lodestar to follow. B. Gerald Cantor, an investment banker, devoted twenty-five years to the exclusive pursuit of Rodin's work. Hundreds of sculptures, drawings, casts, preliminary studies, exhibition posters, letters, calling cards, and other memorabilia formed the largest private collection of the French titan's range of creativity.

❮ WHERE WAS IT MADE?

Although this criterion might seem to impinge on the previous one, which refers to the maker, there is a difference for the discriminating collector whose interest in objects relates to their places of origin.

Not only do citizens or descendants of natives of a country often collect on a national basis, but so also do those whose only ties are those of admiration. Some great collectors of oriental porcelain have never been to the Far East, yet they are interested only in acquiring wares from a specific region.

Provincial museums all over Europe proclaim their local arts and artifacts, as do their private and public counterparts in the United States. Villages and towns, districts, regions, and states proudly present collections based on place of origin.

Regional pride dictates formation of outstanding private collections, which perform historical as well as geographic services. Philadelphia Chippendale furniture, South Carolina or Boston silver, Nailsea glass, Waterford crystal, and Staffordshire, Bennington, or New York pottery are among subjects that have inspired collections created in praise of place.

❮ HOW WAS IT MADE?

Sparked by an attraction to the art or craft rather than the material or function, it is possible for a collection to ride astride technique itself. Beading, quilting, carving, weaving, enameling, and etching, as well as inlay, mosaic, cloisonné, and silhouette are a few of the processes so admired that outstanding examples are sought from the far distant past to the present. Often gifted artists and artisans are the most ardent collectors, understanding and appreciating development and variation of technical modes.

The marvel of the human hand and its capacity for infinite pains and expressive creativity is a never-failing reservoir in which any collector can always find refreshment and inspiration. Every fine-art collection testifies to this, and many collections of contemporary crafts pay homage to skill and technique above all.

Splendid workmanship need not be confined to handwork; adroitly manufactured articles, especially of the early industrial era, inspire collections of paisley shawls, buttons, candlesticks, lamps, toys, and jewelry. The latter, along with both plated and sterling silver objects, were turned out in huge quantities in the late nineteenth century, and their excellent workmanship is a source of fascination, especially in recent times when more complex machines seem to produce less attractive quality.

(TO WHOM DID IT BELONG?

The identity of previous owners forms the rationale for collections of memorabilia. Not all are disposed to be so impressed, but for those who are, association forms a strong initiative for launching a collection.

Autographs, manuscripts, letters, jewelry, clothing, furnishings, and in general the possessions of famous, distinguished, creative, notorious, or historically important figures of minor to major magnitude take on some of the charisma of the owners, powerfully exciting the imagination of the collector.

President Lincoln's waistcoat button and Marie Antoinette's Sevres and ormolu-decorated desk share the distinction of having been owned by famous people; they are separated by the difference between an otherwise ordinary button and an undoubtedly fabulous work of art and craftsmanship worthy of acquisition in its own right.

Some take the high road, some take the low. Both are willing to place value on previous ownership; obviously both can start with a single item and, by choosing it as a basis for commitment, go on to form collections that may be a world apart, but will have the common basis of personal association.

(WHEN WAS IT MADE?

Born in 1930, one man stakes his claim to being a collector because he is acquiring objects that were made or commonly used in that year. His aim is to re-create a 1930 household, complete with books, gadgets, clothing, furniture, and utilitarian and decorative furnishings, in which he lives.

Less devoted to personalized permanent birthday celebration, many form collections that are focused on a particular period or era because they find it worthy of illumination.

Books, coins, stamps, newspapers, and historical and commemorative collections depend largely on date. Authentic period styles are naturally time-connected, and when a collection indicates development and influence, questions of what came first are of primary importance.

Patent dates, sgraffito or scratched dates on pottery, and the date element of silver hallmarks are integral to formation of collections, and archaeological dating cannot be overestimated.

Like the smile the cat left in the tree, date alone is an abstract, but it gathers consequence from its relevance to the place of the object in the scheme of the collection.

Some collectors particularly enjoy the ability to confirm and account for vintage or antique items by dating them accurately or with a reasonably reliable "circa."

(HOW BIG IS IT?

Like the woman whose choice of an anniversary gift was "The biggest diamond at my bridge game," some collectors are motivated by size alone. Huge paintings, massive pieces of furniture, and enormous articles in silver, glass, or ceramic appeal for their grand proportions. They give the collector who has the means to store or display such items the advantage in bargaining, since competition is usually less where size presents a problem in storage and display.

However, throughout the history of collecting, the desire to acquire miniatures has been by far the stronger impulse. Whether as an effigy of reality or as a physically manageable replica of it, preoccupation with collecting the smallest possible version of objects has deep and ancient roots. The peerless temple treasuries of early Greece contained great quantities of miniatures, and they are found in countless archaeological sites in every culture.

More recently, miniature collecting has grown in popularity as a segment of the collecting field. As tiny objects pour forth in mass production and painstaking handcraft, a growing adult market seeks and treasures them in endless variety for doll house, shelf, and vitrine.

Antique miniatures are preferred by one group; this is a most challenging and costly quest for collectors with boundless patience and optimism to match it. It is one thing to require a particular type and size of Georgian antique miniature chandelier, and another matter to find it. In this instance, molehills are more difficult than mountains, but collectors conquer both.

❰ COLOR FACTORS

The passion for a color can be an obsessive and persistent motivation in forming a collection. It may be expressed by acquiring a wide range of objects in the chosen color, which may even be restricted to a particular shade, or it may be as permissible variations of the color, but in a limited range of objects.

Certain colors seem to arouse more excitement than others in this regard, but hardly any are without appeal to some collectors. Subtle or no-color celery green and tones of khaki are sought at one end of the collecting spectrum, while brilliant violets, reds, and greens drive others to accumulate ceramics, glass, textiles, and jewelry.

Collecting by color alone is not common, but many collect specific categories in particular colors. Cranberry glass, celadon china, spinach jade, or black-and-white transfer pottery speak to the interest of color-directed collectors.

❰ STYLE

"I collect Art Deco" or "I collect Eastlake" are expressions of commitment to a style. Some who collect along these lines have functional decorative interests in whatever style they have chosen and will set about to assemble room settings. However, there are many smaller-scaled projects that can serve to program style-focused collections, appealing to the collector with a preference for a period's design expressions.

Victorian pincushions, Chippendale tea caddies, Jacobean embroideries, French Provincial textiles, Georgian Sheffield, and Art Deco cigarette boxes can spark and satisfy the urge to follow a particular period within restricted channels.

⟨ SUBJECT MATTER

While choice of subject matter often lies in the depth of the collector's personality and might have to be pursued into the unconscious for the sources of appeal, it is a strong contender for priority in directing the formation of collections.

As expressed in the sculptural form of the utilitarian object, as in the cow-figure creamer, heart-shaped picture frame, lion-masqued doorknocker, or flower-contoured vase, subject is a very popular foundation for collections.

Ornamentally employed, shells, flowers, fruit, vegetables, botanicals, human and animal figures as well as geometrics, lyres, ships, and other conventional or unusual subjects will shape collections by virtue of their forms. Often the decoration on the ceramic, textile, glass, or other material will be what is collected.

Known as iconography in painting, graphics, and sculpture, subject is often used symbolically to express ideas and emotions—sometimes, depending on the culture and context, several different ones. Thus the unicorn might represent the hunt for perfection, religious sacrifice, or sex symbolism. However, on a simpler level, landscape, still-life, portrait, and domestic scenes present subject matter more directly, and are collected accordingly.

Although not considered sculpture, purely decorative figures in ceramics, glass, precious or base metal, ivory and semiprecious or precious stone are usually collected with reference to subject.

⟨ THEME AND VIEWPOINT

As the connective tissue that transcends yet binds motive and matter, both theme and viewpoint build collections, shape them,

determine their size, and, in general, distinguish the collector from
the packrat.

From ancient times it has been a custom for buildings, monu-
ments, and statuary to carry inscriptions denoting the purpose and
aim to which they are dedicated. Called an epigraph, such words
are usually chiseled or mounted as the finishing touches, but actually they originate before the first sketch or blueprint has been
made.

Whether or not it is called by a name, a real collection always
has an epigraph. Before a nucleus of objects, cut glass, silver
spoons, cups and saucers, music boxes, or vintage autos is vali-
dated as a collection in formation, this first step must be taken, its
creator having planned what the show will tell. Aside from other
purposes of the collection, which may include status, security, ap-
peasement of superstition, or desire for profit, establishment of
directions and goals intrinsic to the collection itself are required.

The individuality and originality of collectors finds natural expression through theme and viewpoint. One collection of candlesnuffers illustrates the ingenuity of devices with which candles
were extinguished when they were a lighting source of major importance. A second collection of candlesnuffers proclaims the
workmanship of the outstanding English silversmiths of the eighteenth and early nineteenth centuries. The first collection says,
"How cleverly candlesnuffers were designed"; the second collection says, "What extraordinary workmanship was lavished on
Georgian silver candlesnuffers." Something has also been said
about the two collectors.

Collections of sports trophies are not uncommon, but theme
and viewpoint give a certain grandeur to a collection of old
punching bags, marked with the names of the fighters who trained
on them. Battered, sweat- and time-stained, discolored, and hanging limply in rows, they are marked with the poignancy of both
defeat and victory and say more about boxing than the most glamorous collection of trophies ever could.

Having formed an excellent collection of 1876 U.S. centennial
material, a collector next turned to bicentennial commemoratives.
The interesting result was a sensitive comparison between the exu-
berant and optimistic centennial and the obviously more serious
bicentennial.

One collector acquires only fakes. Paintings must be identified as having been made with intent to falsify, and the goal is to attribute them to the faker source. When a purchase turned out to be authentic, it was quickly sold, having no place in this collection, the theme of which is, "Only authentic fakes."

A collection of vintage Fords comments smugly, "Slower was better," while another of custom cars made before 1930 says, "Engineering is an art."

The *Hindenburg* disaster still fascinates collectors who seek anything associated with the ill-fated zeppelin airship. The theme and viewpoint, "Even such a splendid balloon may burst," speaks of more than this particular tragic accident.

Collections of military helmets, postcards, Christmas tree ornaments, lithophanes, beer trays, tokens, trivets, and bread plates tell us not only about themselves, but also comment on values and customs. By looking into another time or culture, we gain insight into our own and ourselves.

Whether or not the collector starts out with a viewpoint, the collection often takes on a life and momentum of its own. In Rotterdam, Dr. Van der Poel, intrigued with the history of taxes, went about to form a collection to illustrate it. It has grown into a private museum of twenty rooms, which includes an international selection of five thousand cartoons on taxes, tax receipts from Egyptian times on, a complete collection of tax stamps, a large assortment of ingenious devices for smuggling, and paintings and prints about taxes, including the Rembrandt "Tribute" etching. In its growth, this collection expanded to express the universal responses of fear, aversion, and ingenuity in avoidance of taxes, a theme and viewpoint with variations.

Any collection can become interesting; how nearly it approaches greatness depends on what it "believes."

Theme and viewpoint present no problems for certain corporations when they decide to form collections to promote and publicize a particular product. The Campbell Soup Company's choice of soup tureens for the firm's collection and museum would seem as obligatory as it is logical; obviously the importance of the containers indicates that soup has always ranked high in prestige as well as subsistence value.

The remarkable array of full-bodied containers in a wide range of materials and forms is as varied as it is handsome and completely suitable for its corporate purpose, with inferences of hospitable plenty.

This need not overwhelm the modest soup lover who might wish to form a collection offering homage to the potage that pleases peasant and potentate. It could be accomplished with soup ladles and soup spoons, and in either case, an original and worthwhile collection could be assembled, provided the theme and viewpoint were reinforced by the selections.

CHAPTER 4

GUIDELINES FOR DECISIONS

- HELPFUL STANDARDS - AVAILABILITY
- VARIETY - IDENTIFIABILITY
- MEASURE OF QUALITY
- PROVABLE AUTHENTICITY
- DESIRABLE ORIGINS
- IS THERE A CONTINUING MARKET?
- GROWTH VALUE POTENTIAL - FLEXIBILITY
- HOW REPRODUCIBLE? - NOW OR THEN?
- APPRAISE YOUR CAPACITY
- SOURCES FOR GUIDANCE

ONE REACHES THE shore of the Rubicon, which divides casual from serious collectors, imperceptibly, possibly unconsciously, having been conveyed by character, personality, mentality, and circumstance. Up to this point, the collection may have chosen its maker; now the collector must decide not only on this or another subject, but also specifically on the nature, contours, and theme of a collection.

(HELPFUL STANDARDS

Whether or not aware of the possible pitfalls, few feel equipped to undertake the hazards of this commitment without assistance. Not knowing, or perhaps trusting dealers who might be helpful, lacking access to the private experts and scholars of the rich, as well as their ability to finance mistakes, many fledgling collectors are frustrated and discouraged. No matter how often exhorted to acquire what they "love," they are fearful of not being able to sustain the relationship for better or worse, should the acquisitions prove unworthy. Lacking a set of guidelines so basic and universal that it would aid in forming any and every kind of collection, large numbers of would-be collectors remain desultory packrats or undertake prepackaged "limited edition" ersatz collections that smother and destroy any spark of creativity.

To remedy this, some guidelines have been garnered from the wisdom of veteran collectors and dealers, as well as scholars and museum experts. They are presented, not as a formula, but as a standard by which to make, as well as measure, an individual pattern or design for collecting, one that will have the best chance for growth, development, and fruition, a practical program with realistic goals.

(AVAILABILITY

If an item is so rare that few are known to exist, the likelihood of forming a viable collection is minimal. Give yourself a fair chance and choose a subject that will reward search and will allow scope for your ideas in molding it into a collection.

Although the possibility of even a mad magnate planning to form a collection of Vermeer paintings of which less than forty are known, most of them in museums, is remote; on a more accessible level, there are some seashells known in fewer than a dozen examples. Of course, there is always the possibility that thousands more will turn up in a harvest, but that is a chancy note on which to plan a specialized collection. Similarly, if most known examples of a category are owned by institutions, this would also be an obvious hazard, despite the predilection of some to deaccession.

When the collection is based on a predetermined framework such as a series or a catalog, the lack of a key piece is a serious obstacle. For collectors of official presidential inaugural medals, such a key item is the 1905 Theodore Roosevelt specimen struck in bronze by Tiffany. Only 120 were made, and they rarely appear on the market, one brought forty-five hundred dollars at auction in 1974, shortly following a "wanted to buy" advertisement, offering twelve hundred dollars. Prudent collectors try to evaluate in advance the odds that rarity will be a crippling factor in forming a closed series.

In general, for ambitious collectors, medium rare is best; while for the more prudent, plentiful Victorian jewelry, contemporary graphics, opera recordings, and other open-ended than serially obligatory items can be rewarding.

(VARIETY

A sufficiency of disparate examples within the category is required for a well-balanced collection. No more than horseshoes do identical records, vases, buckles, or hatpins comprise a collection. This is not to underestimate the charms of rarity; certain items will always be scarcer than others. However, the kind of thing collected must present a panorama that makes an interesting statement. Tin tobacco advertising tags, of which three thousand have been identified as a start, illustrate potential opportunity with viable variety. Areas in the fields of coins and stamps, bottles, candle holders, buttons, books, and autographs are literally open-ended for collectors.

Windsor chairs in their seemingly endless variety, hand-carved decoy ducks, each individually reflecting the combination of the hand of the carver with the eye of the hunter; different models of vintage typewriters, iceboxes, even orange juicers, have been formed into complete collections because of the multiplicity of their versions.

A collector of American Chippendale furniture would be deliriously happy to find a single hairy-pawed example; but since only half a dozen pieces with such legs have surfaced in a thirty-year period, and it is thought that perhaps two dozen were made about the period of the American Revolution, it seems unlikely that anyone would consider setting up as a collector of this shaggy-pawed specialty, even though six-figure prices might not daunt him or her in the search for any such piece.

❴ IDENTIFIABILITY

A distinctive profile, or at least a single readily recognizable characteristic should define the subject of a collection. A lock of hair from each United States President might form a collection suitable for a barber college, but its other limitations are obvious when compared to a set of presidential autographs.

In the field of art, style, subject, color, brushwork, or some aspect of technique will distinguish work of consequence, and even though there was a period when Picasso and Bracque seemed to be working in an interchangeable cubist style, collectors of cubism find no fault with having some of each, since in that case, they are collecting the identifiable style as expounded by two masters.

How then is it possible to justify collecting Coca-Cola bottles when so many millions of identical pieces were mass produced? Here the answer lies again in the purpose of the collection. Since by 1913, other firms had come into the market with substitutions similar to the straight-sided bottle the firm had been using since 1894, it was decided to differentiate from the competition by patenting a new bottle with a bulged center, the basis for future variations. Thus a complete collection would include an example of each *kind* of Coca-Cola bottle from 1894 to the present.

Certain subjects, such as Hudson River Valley School paintings, Chinese propaganda posters, Kentucky rifles, Mary Gregory glass, and Wedgwood's basalt stoneware, have strongly identifiable characteristics that can be spotted across a crowded room, shop, or museum gallery, while others, equally individual, require closer scrutiny. In any case, experienced collectors arrange to avoid possible confusion between an item sought and one somewhat similar.

⟪ MEASURE OF QUALITY

Quality has several facets in reference to collecting. One of them is a cast system of rating categories in such a way as to place collections of Tiffany glass on a higher level than Carnival, Depression, or Heisey glass, which in their turn rate in order. Sevres ranks above Limoges china and Early American above Victorian silver, while prestigious Impressionist paintings overshadow the Hudson River School.

Some of this is based on snobbery, some on economics and market value, some on antiquity as priority, some on workmanship, artistry, or taste. Its defenders acknowledge only their own versions of what constitutes quality.

However, if temperament, psychology, economics, chance, and circumstance are acknowledged to play consequential roles, this aspect of quality can be recognized, if not recommended, as a guideline. Even in terms of investment, as we have noted and shall further observe, it may not be the most desirable formula to follow.

The true importance of standard of quality is its presence within the confines of any collection, and the one that grows out of the objectives and goals. Condition, origin, authenticity, finish, technique, and rarity in varying degrees and combination will define the quality of collections of spittoons or diamond coronets.

Evenness of quality in a collection is the third facet, and while a collector's reach will usually exceed the grasp, constant culling for improvement is a continuing activity.

⟪ PROVABLE AUTHENTICITY

Absolute reliance on marks, labels, and signatures just isn't realistic. However, those who wish to collect ceramics, paintings, clocks, watches, silver, art glass, and certain other categories must master marks in the early stages of forming a collection in order not to be dependent on them later.

Experts establish the validity of marks by their satisfaction with the piece in itself, first checking material, design, workmanship, or ornament as characteristic. If the items pass prior tests, then the marks are evaluated. Beginners collecting in a field where marks are important are urged to learn to collate marks with the merits of each piece. Leaning on marks alone is a little learning, and hence the most dangerous kind.

Whatever may be required to establish authenticity, be it pedigree, previous ownership, intrinsic aspects that are subjective, or objective scientific testing, the wise collector plays by the rules of the category. The assurance of authenticity is more inherent in some collectibles than others. Certain types of glass simply cannot be positively attributed unless they are found buried under the foundations of a glass house. An unsigned netsuke or weathervane has to be taken in stride. It is the exception that can be attributed in many fields in which anonymity rules.

(DESIRABLE ORIGINS

Theft of antiques and collectibles as well as art works has become a commonplace, and almost every issue of every publication devoted to them features stories, lists, or advertisements devoted to alerting collectors and dealers about such incidents.

In addition, archaeological material, surreptitiously excavated and then smuggled, is constantly offered to private collectors as it is to museums and dealers. Beginning collectors are especially urged to require a clear title in the form of a bill that further takes the responsibility for the purchase being legally salable.

Antiquities make special demands; ancient pottery may indeed have been excavated from an Etruscan tomb or Mayan ruin, but unless indubitably traced, its origins are forever questionable, as is its value in the formation of a collection.

Traceable ownership adds allure by a process of accretion, as a painting or object moves from one important collection to another. Just to have been part of one well-known and well-regarded collection makes a piece more desirable.

Estates that have not yet been settled, dual or group ownership can also create problems if one has had the misfortune to make a purchase that the vendor was not authorized to sell.

An example indicating that there is more than one way to skin a cat occurred upon the death of the great photographer Margaret Bourke-White. Her will bequeathed all the photographs and negatives in her possession to Syracuse University. Apparently the house was incompletely cleared before being sold, as files that had been cached behind closets were found later. A person who claimed to have been offered such material by possibly unauthorized parties is said to have reported this to the university, and to have received a number of Bourke-White items out of its now enormous archive as a reward.

❲ IS THERE A CONTINUING MARKET?

Liquidity must be considered if the investment in the collection is a factor in your net worth. For those whose collections consist of "souvenir" ashtrays from hotels or restaurants, the concern about a market will be negligible. However, in most cases prudent collectors of all economic strata want to know whether they can readily convert their treasures to cash in an emergency.

It is easier to buy than to sell. Where, when, and how to sell should be considered before a serious commitment is made to a costly collection.

❲ GROWTH VALUE POTENTIAL

Watching the cycles of interest in the cavalcade of collectibles, old-timers recommend that the "in" fields be avoided because they are overpriced, usually rife with fakes, and oversought. They suggest entering less fashionable areas or those yet unexplored. Trail-blazing gives the collector of limited means the opportunity to be creative and form outstanding collections. Typewriters, butter molds, and match safes have recently illustrated this, while a period when Chinese enamels interested few was obviously the time to pursue them.

More items costing five dollars will increase to fifty dollars than will five-thousand-dollar pieces increase to fifty thousand dollars. The ratio comes down as the figures go up. On the other hand, veterans believe that prime, first-quality, important, and obviously costlier collectibles will retain value more securely in times of economic distress. It would seem that there might be some place on a chart where the point of diminishing returns shrinks or stops the potential growth in monetary value of a five-million-dollar painting.

❨ FLEXIBILITY

Some experts advise collectors to keep two shafts in their bows. During occasional short or even long intervals when nothing suitable can be acquired for one collection, you can swing to the other. This is said to keep the standard high for both and to make you less vulnerable to be held up for gunpoint prices.

A limited project should permit the possibility of expansion to include another associated unit in which the momentum from the first can be employed. Whenever one collection can become a module unit of a larger one, the resulting advantage is the enhancement of each and the added experience of the creator. Having formed a thimble collection, one can move on to sewing birds.

❨ HOW REPRODUCIBLE?

In general, reproductions horrify collectors whose only interest is to identify and thus avoid them. In choosing a field in which to specialize, collectors have long been urged to stay away from those that have been invaded by reproductions. This has become increasingly difficult, but increasingly worthwhile.

When widespread reproduction has taken place, especially in such difficult areas as American milk glass, African primitive art, American Indian jewelry, graphics, and rare coins, those who enter must be prepared to beware and realize that eventually the burden of proof of authenticity may be shifted to them.

❨ NOW OR THEN?

One school of collectors prefers its artists or artisans long gone, believing that death provides a firm foundation on which to form a collection. The existing work cannot be added to, but must inevitably diminish, and rarity will add an extra dimension to embellish whatever intrinsic values motivated the collection. A contrary opinion is held by those envisioning improvement and appreciation in the work of living artists or craftsmen. They hope either to add later work when it is accomplished, or that the collection,. as is, will gain in reflected glory.

Obsolescence of workmanship or material, or a combination of both is a recommended attraction by those who believe that seaweed marquetry, Boulle inlay, warming pans, aleshoes, argand lamps, and jet or steel jewelry cannot but form worthwhile collections by reason of having become archaic objects.

⟨ APPRAISE YOUR CAPACITY

A profound material passion for the collection combined with a strong emotional attachment is the ideal motivation, yet it may not be able to overcome mundane obstacles. In choosing what the individual will collect it may be necessary to resist categories that are too fragile, costly, difficult to find, or impossible to store safely, handle conveniently, or liquidate profitably.

Prudence dictates that certain considerations be explored in advance. If delicate glassware and porcelain cannot be protected; if your house is exposed to thieves and you cannot get sufficient insurance coverage for valuables; if damp, dust, and sunlight cannot be controlled, your choices become limited. Ironically, guns, those instruments of belligerence, need extraordinary protection, as they are exceptionally tempting targets for theft. Coins and stamps that cannot be readily identified as yours offer safety problems as well.

Some items age less gracefully than others; silk or ivory fans, graphics, and leather require special atmospheric considerations, as does veneered furniture.

Veterans like to know what can be repaired, how much it will cost, and how repaired items are evaluated. If repairs can be completely masked, it is good for the seller, dangerous for the buyer. It is important to know if tests are available. These are factors to govern decisions, based as much on the facts as on the collector's response to them.

Computers may be more or less successful in mating individuals, and perhaps someday they will be used to match collectors with collections; in the meantime, these guidelines should be helpful. Related to the advice that it is just as easy to fall in love with a rich, attractive person, some of the above is materially oriented to point out those features to the courting collector.

❲ SOURCES FOR GUIDANCE

The choice of what kind of a collection to form need not be agonizing, but it should be seriously undertaken with a view to long-term as well as immediate satisfactions. The commitment need not be considered binding for life; like most it is made for the foreseeable future, subject to the vagaries of taste and fortune, with hopes for a lifetime relationship.

In the search for a worthy and compatible commitment, aspiring collectors can also consult with specialist dealers who cater to collectors and can offer practical suggestions. Talking with collecting club officers or members, visits to auctions and observation of advertising trends, together with attention of current magazine articles and classic and new books on collecting will be helpful.

Guidance may come from museum collections and exhibitions and from museum staff members. Curators dream of collectors they can influence, and while they hope for generous and wealthy donors of masterpieces, they realistically settle for less as they cast their bread upon the waters of intelligent inquiry from neophytes.

Collections are often exhibited, although many shows and exhibitions do not consist of just a single collection. In a sense, many exhibitions in museums and galleries are idealized collections, with only the fleeting existence of a passing occasion. In general, exhibitions are useful to both new and veteran collectors; both can learn from the organizer's intent to create an uncommon statement of value and interest.

CHAPTER 5

ANATOMY OF YOUR COLLECTION

❨ MAKING THE PLAN ❨ COMPARATIVES
❨ CHANGING FORMS ❨ POINTS
❨ CATALOGS AND SETS ❨ TEXTBOOK MODELS
❨ DERIVATIVE
❨ MASTERPIECE OR MASTERWORK
❨ COUNTERCULTURE ❨ ECLECTIC
❨ AFFINITY ❨ NEW PERSPECTIVES
❨ CULTURAL MATRIX ❨ KEYSTONE
❨ RETROSPECTIVE ❨ EXOTICA
❨ SELF-GROUPING ❨ TUTORIAL
❨ WHEN IS ENOUGH?

COLLECTIONS ORIGINATE in ideas and emotions—something sparks the imagination and sets off the chain of events that leads to formation of a collection, but whether it will consist of a dozen pieces or several thousand, it requires a plan at some point in its formation if it is to be a cohesive whole and not a formless jumble. This plan is really a system of relationships, which is also the technique for acquisition. The material accumulated must be assimilated so the collection has healthy growth in the direction of its aims and purpose.

(MAKING THE PLAN

Some collectors create a design without making a formal blueprint. Like that character who was amazed to find that he spoke in prose, they are unaware that they have been using established techniques. However, whether set down in advance in formal fashion or unconsciously sketched, it is the program that will determine how far the collection will go and how successfully it will get there.

The different systems are not mutually exclusive—some mesh harmoniously together; in this case, one is usually dominant, giving the collection its character.

(COMPARATIVES

Comparison may collate or confront, may point up similarities or differences. A collection of nutcrackers illustrating many different methods of crushing nutshells compares the functions of a nutcracker as a tool. Another collection of two-pronged nutcrackers would emphasize the variations in the same basic design. Each collection would be comparing different aspects of nutcrackers.

Valentines from various countries, fashion magazines separated by decades, flower paintings of many different styles, and cosmetic containers from different cultures are among the countless objects especially suitable for comparative presentation with the purpose of illustrating the differences vis-à-vis one another.

A stamp collector using music as the theme could employ the comparative method by selecting those stamps that have paid homage to Beethoven, to national composers, to international conductors and singers, or to musical institutions and by showing how each country's issues expressed some national approach.

The Metropolitan Museum of Art had over fifty drawings by Goya, a nearly complete set of his prints, and the largest, most representative selection of his oils outside Madrid, including superb masterpieces. Yet museum officials jumped at an opportunity to acquire another Goya painting, a portrait of a child, for the purpose of juxtaposing it with another child's portrait by the same artist. This provided an opportunity for comparison that would show Goya in one case as a poetic eighteenth-century painter, and in another as a profoundly moving realist.

ℂ CHANGING FORMS

That only immutable, change, fascinates collectors as it does all inquiring minds. The collector so inclined aims to show the altering aspect of objects, be it as evolution, development, or deterioration. The important purpose is to follow the various stages.

Obviously there is much grist for this mill. The works of nature show their evolutionary changes over millennia, as collections of fossils may be organized to testify. Even if a form, such as the Chinese tripod, seems to defy time and alteration, careful study will show that the law of change is inexorable, that variations do occur, and the collection will reflect it.

Products of the Industrial Revolution—cameras, typewriters, alarm clocks, and more recently small calculators—are being collected in serial form to show their development.

Almost any subject can be collected in this fashion, from perfume bottles to suits of armor, and it may cover a short span of time or take the long, panoramic view; the collector may choose the most appropriate viewpoint.

In addition to the objects themselves, many materials *about* the changing forms make collections. Catalogs, advertisements, patent papers, order forms, labels, and business cards are among the collectible items that show the existence of various versions and their development.

❪ POINTS

Selection by details or secondary features known as points gives its name to this often-employed method of forming a collection.

Glass decanters chosen for the variation of neck rings, brass candlesticks for the placement of bobeches or drip disks, and ceramics selected for butterfly, cupid, or bowknot decorations variously illustrate such a blueprint.

Bottle collectors who focus on the retention of the original contents, be they medicines or soft drinks; stamp collectors who require only that the stamp have a bilingual text; and the collector of Chinese ceramics that must have French ormolu mounts of the eighteenth century, give the secondary characteristic primary importance.

Slot machines are collected with reference to the point, which is usually the pay or jackpot arrangement. The reserve jackpot, the "golden" token, free-play or "futurity" machines, loss cancellation systems, and payouts in merchandise such as cigarettes or golf balls form the classification framework for such collections.

❪ CATALOGS AND SETS

Filling in a stamp album, acquiring each item on a page or section of a turn-of-the-century Sears, Roebuck catalog or manufacturer's or jobber's handbook is a form of collecting that may center on toys, barber bottles, or napkin rings, but is essentially the catalog pattern of collecting. Because some collectors have insisted on literally finding exactly each item listed, searching with dogged energy, it has been discovered that some of these catalogs were printed before the manufacturing process had been completed, hence were not always accurate. However, they are still used as road maps, despite occasional detours.

Consecutive issues, such as annual Christmas plates, Indian head pennies, presidential medals, advertising cards, and opera programs fall into the category of collecting by sets. Flatware or dinnerware services, sets of books, dressing table or toilet sets, sets of coins, and sets of commercial limited editions, the latter made to be collected as sets, can be defined as collections.

One collector who claims to have every work designed by Dali in a multiple output, including postcards, color print slides of paintings, signed, unsigned, and "unlimited" graphics, plates and medallions, tapestries, neckties, puzzles, stamps, and coins, has created an unlimited one-man catalog.

❨ TEXTBOOK MODELS

When the collector uses as model the classification and arrangement of a published text, it is referred to as a textbook collection. In a scholarly illustration, Bernard Rackham's *Guide to Italian Maiolica*, a general survey of the subject by the keeper of the Department of Ceramics of the Kensington Museum might be said to be an example, giving the collector who aims to form a representative group on this subject, a scaffolding on which to build.

In the upper echelons of collecting, the expression "textbook collection" implies that it is good but not original and might be considered by some to contain a faint hint of reproach. However, the neophyte collector who follows a textbook, be it in cut glass, Weller pottery, or pocket knives, is getting a good education indeed, and may be blazing trails into future originality.

❨ DERIVATIVE

During the Victorian era almost every style of the past served as inspiration and was redesigned into some aspect of the decorative arts. It amuses some to collect Victorian versions of Gothic, Tudor, any of the French Louis, Renaissance, Moorish, or Jacobean. Some of the most interesting collections aim to show recurring influences, whether of style, design, or subject; Greek classicism has reappeared in many eras from Roman times to ours, always in a translation clearly to be read as to the source.

A collection of French early-twentieth-century prints showing the influences of Japanese woodcuts is an outstanding example of derivatively programmed collecting, as is a collection of French sculpture pointing to its African influences.

Great and famous reproductions of masterpieces were once highly regarded as forming worthwhile collections; even today, "from the school of" indicating that the work was influenced by leading creators is not an unworthy subject for excellent collections, frankly structured to show derivative influences.

⟨ MASTERPIECE OR MASTERWORK

Too often collectors think in terms of the greatest names in the fine arts as sole creators of masterpieces, convinced that if they cannot aspire to such as Rembrandt, they must forget their starry dreams.

Obviously, those who can afford to collect generally recognized glamorous masterpieces of fine art are few; however, there are outstanding masterworks still within the reach of many in areas that have not been preclassified. If the expression "masterwork" is substituted for "masterpiece," its meaning is defined as the work of a master or expert. Thus the scope is expanded to include work of the quality that crowns an artisan's as well as an artist's output, and the opportunity to acquire a collection of masterpieces does not seem so remote.

Embroidery, musical instruments, silhouettes, fish slices, case glass, medals, even a segment of a suit of armor may qualify as material for masterwork collections, giving self-styled minor collectors major successes. In this connection, it must also be remembered that masterpieces are often redefined within decades, and collectors are largely responsible for doing so.

⟨ COUNTERCULTURE

It may be hard to believe, but it is true that just as some strive to acquire the best examples, so there has been a trend to form collections of "the worst," not only in taste, but also in quality of workmanship and design.

Originating in the 1960s and labeled "camp," it started as an interest in the outrageous as a nonconformist effort to create shock and satirize serious collecting. Overornate and disparate ornament, garish or dreary colors, unbalanced and inept forms, almost anything sufficiently flashy from glass coasters to picture frames, furniture, and clothing was singled out for approval and acquisition. Some of it, mislabeled Art Deco, was worlds away from the finely crafted, sleekly shaped design in rich materials, characteristic of the best of that period. The "dreadful" fancier sought out mass-produced "junktiques" of the twentieth century or late nineteenth, in almost any category.

Properly labeled "counterculture" collecting, it is not collecting against the fashion, but literally against any established standards, and in sophisticated circles, served as a chic amusement. However, many naïve dealers and collectors took seriously what was intended as a joke on them, and a large segment of the establishment collects costly freaks rather than penny dreadfuls, because it has become big business.

⟨ ECLECTIC

A convenient cover for sins of confusion, this method of collecting without boundaries of time, place, period, or design brings splendid results when there is an over-all guiding plan with reference to its purpose.

Its officers having decided to form an art collection, a Chicago bank put the task into the hands of veteran art curator and critic Katherine Kuh, who immediately wrote out a program of what she thought the collection should be. It would be "Formed from material of all periods, all places, and of the highest quality, with a single standard of taste."

Six years and twenty-three hundred items of painting, sculpture, drawings, prints, tapestries, and other objects later, it included a Japanese screen of circa 1800, a Bourdelle bronze, a Roman portrait bust, Coptic art, a sixth-century B.C. Greek helmet, a nineteenth-century *trompe l'oeil* painting, a Gilbert Stuart portrait, and African masks. Its purpose, to decorate the bank's offices, has been richly fulfilled, and, according to bank authorities, at the cost of less than one first-class Renoir painting. The costly modern artists, Arp, Calder, Noguchi, Miro, and Picasso appear in prints, small drawings, and tapestries.

Another example of the eclectic method appears in the collection formed by Mr. and Mrs. B. Alastair Martin, known as the Guennol Collection. Relics of the Romanovs, Nigerian, Amerindian, pre-Columbian, Far Eastern, postmedieval, American folk art, ancient Greek, Egyptian, and Near Eastern are included. A group entitled Enigmatic—of unknown provenance and origin—further characterizes the imaginative activity of collectors under the eclectic banner.

⟮ AFFINITY

When Mr. and Mrs. Charles Wrightsman, whose internationally admired collection of eighteenth-century French furniture and decorations included a Renoir "in the eighteenth-century taste," it was no error, but an example of collecting by affinity.

Fine French Furniture, known as FFF, the cream of eighteenth-century French craftsmanship and artistry, has the qualities that attract rich perfectionist collectors; they may be capricious, but not in this connection. This is not merely the expression of taste, but also of a bond that transcends time and place as well as design and style, such as matching a four-thousand-year-old Cycladic head with a 1920 Modigliani sculpture, or a 600 B.C. Scythian gold ornament with an Irish silver brooch of A.D. 500.

Affinity makes for strange and interesting collections; there are many sorts of ties and interconnections that may structure them. Disparate objects from different cultures and centuries may belong together in a collection if they are related by mood and spirit.

⟮ NEW PERSPECTIVES

Every era wears its own spectacles, and collectors seeing old forms in new guises develop new guidelines. When Windsor chairs are collected as sculptured forms, quilts as wall hangings, trivets as pure design, and bookends as bas-reliefs, it is the opposite of cutesy transformations of antiques for neo-utility. Any automobile crushed to render it disposable is suddenly seen as an art form, and it is collected quite differently from the vintage automobile. Old photographs are seen in a novel context; technique as well as subject take on interest for a new generation of collectors who literally "resee."

The art collectors who buy "letters of intention" of artists who explain a conceptual project that need never be started have been led to new perspectives of collecting—they acquire "concepts" and the "positive proof" that the artist put the idea on paper and signed it. At first, dealers were apprehensive over this new approach, but having developed a technique for collectors to buy something, some are encouraging it. The intangible or token can now be collected as art!

⟨ CULTURAL MATRIX

A collector of the graphics of Toulouse Lautrec further evokes the atmosphere of the Belle Époque by furnishing his suburban home with Art Nouveau furniture, lamps, glass, ceramics, bronzes, and suitable objects of art. The artist's schoolbooks, bibelots, and most of his letters are included in this excellent example of a collection in its cultural matrix. Those who steep themselves in a period or style find that many advantages accrue from collecting in this fashion, not the least of which is domestic life with the era they particularly love.

Sometimes the cultural matrix *is* the collection, at its best; this technique is artfully varied to combine furniture, paintings, and sculpture with fabrics of the period, wallpapers, silver, and books, more or less simulating a household with a natural interrelation of the meeting of objects of a utilitarian and decorative character.

An outstanding cultural collection now in the Newark Museum was formed by a missionary, earlier in this century. Dr. A. L. Shelton acquired Tibetan sculpture, paintings, ceremonial gear, household objects, and documentary photographs as well as ritual trumpets, butter lamps, magical and astrological implements, cards, traders' and herders' costumes, saddles and harness, weapons and utensils, and even a picnic tent to show his countrymen how remarkably different were these extraordinary people and their way of life.

❲ KEYSTONE

In his introduction to a catalog, *The Art of Oceania, Africa, and the Americas,* Robert Goldwater writes of the search for "prototypical" works against which to measure all others, and surely nothing is more characteristic of an outstanding collection than its success in presenting them.

The definitive work may or may not qualify as a masterpiece, but it may be more important than one in the context of a collection. It usually marks the consummation of a new point of departure in the range of an artist. It may be the first of a series, but it need not be. The model of the first typewriter seems to have been lost, but the Sholes and Glidden model made at Ilion by Remington qualifies as such a keystone piece.

A prototypical work is not a typical example; it is the one by which typical examples can be measured and usually on which they are based. Marking some germinal or seminal point, it serves as the focus for a collection. A selection of only typical examples is unlikely to form an interesting collection, lacking the excitement generated by the presence of keystone pieces.

❲ RETROSPECTIVE

Usually serving to express a survey of an artist's lifework or over a given period when a certain style predominated in the work, the retrospective form is literally what it purports to be, a review, most often used for exhibition purposes in museums and galleries. Yet it need not be limited to the work of an artist or school; such a review may form the scaffolding for a collection of any subject the individual chooses.

Playing cards, maps, guns, hornbooks, clocks, and bottles are among items that lend themselves to such consideration, as well as the work of individual artists or artisans and the output of workshops or factories.

Just as retrospectives of artists often change their generally accepted image, so the object retrospective gives the collector an opportunity to be creative in offering an original viewpoint about the chosen subject.

❲ EXOTICA

Throughout the Middle Ages the *wunderkammer*, the curio chamber next door to the alchemist's laboratory, was the repository for all strange and unusual objects the collector acquired. These might be unicorn horns, coconuts, or emeralds; whatever was curious or grotesque qualified along with the valuable. As we have noted, this simplistic type of collecting has long been out of fashion.

However, an acceptable quest for the unusual and curious will probably always manage to retain some place in the field of collecting, especially if it conforms to a manageable classification.

One collector acquires exceptional single wine glasses ranging from the uncommon to the curious, strange, and bizarre. No "ordinary" wine glass is acceptable, and as the collection grows, additions become increasingly singular.

Hand mirrors, perfume bottles, fans, and doorknockers are among the countless subjects that can be collected according to this method, a limited but satisfying one.

❲ SELF-GROUPING

Some collections present themselves with intrinsic outlines, as a total unit. In art, the American Ashcan School, consisting of seven artists whose work and outlook interlocked, or the Blue Rider German Expressionist group, similarly connected, give the collector such a form to follow.

In the case of a Connecticut family by the name of Ives, whose connections included toy manufacturers, the Ives of Currier & Ives, the clockmakers Ives, leading tool manufacturers and camera pioneers, the collector who wishes to exploit this has predetermined boundaries within which to roam.

Families of English silversmiths often form the framework for collections, as in the case of the Batemans. Widows who took over their husbands' trade and worked as silversmiths give added direction and feminist interest along these lines.

⟨ TUTORIAL

Since museum collections strive for the high points of each art or craft, study collections are the province of the private collector or school. Particular attention to examples that may be less than perfect, but that serve to teach greater appreciation for the best is a worthy purpose, rarely the aim of ambitious collectors.

An outstanding example of such a study collection is that formed by B. Gerald Cantor, whose Rodin collection has been ranked second only to the Rodin Museum in Paris and was so exhaustive that when part of it was given by the collector to Stanford University, it was hailed as a teaching treasure.

Lifetime casts by different foundries balance those of posthumous origin; aborted works, partial figures, and studies for figures were included. Students can compare the same figure in plaster and bronze and observe the works that have been enlarged or reduced in scale by Rodin's assistants. Works made with Rodin's consent in unlimited editions by commercial outlets can be compared with a fine casting of the original realized by Rodin himself. The combination of density and quality are added to by memorabilia, letters, autographs, pictures, objects Rodin owned, and a collection of monographs, catalogs, and books dating back to the nineteenth century. Tutorial collections are not favored by leading museums, yet they are essential to a true understanding of every field of collecting and sought by teaching institutions which look to private collectors to form them.

⟨ WHEN IS ENOUGH?

Even the most disciplined individuals who otherwise run their lives with iron control often become split personalities in the role of collector as passionate desire wars with restraint. The size of

every collection has its own logic, and as search and research un-
cover items that literally "belong," the collection makes its own
demands. Motivated by quality standards as well as realistic limitations, the competent collector culls and discards, as much to
make room as to shape and balance.

The lack of money that may keep a collection from swelling to
outsize proportions can be an advantage in keeping it within reduced and discriminating boundaries. In some cases, the size is
controlled by the method. Storage problems, standards of perfect
condition, and self-limiting catalog and group collections also
serve to cut down accumulation.

Having the funds to "warehouse" plays a role in the size of a
collection. Capacity for pleasure deferred as well as willingness to
invest in storage charges kept much of the twelve-thousand-piece
Hirshhorn art collection growing through decades when the collector had to make periodic visits to a "gloomy jungle" in some
warehouse to see some of his treasures. Robert Scull claimed that
the only time he ever saw his entire collection of pop art at one
time was at the exhibition at the auction gallery where it was
finally dispersed.

A time plan for forming a collection, sometimes possible, as
with limited editions, or necessary, as when funds are available
only at stated intervals, also forms a boundary in relation to size.
Time span is a territory too, whether set by circumstances in or
beyond the collector's control.

CHAPTER 6

EXPLORING BASIC RESOURCES

- "THE TRADE" GOLDEN FLEECE
- PATTERNS OF DISTRIBUTION
- PRIVATE DEALERS
- PRIVATE CONSULTANTS
- SPECIALIST DEALERS
- GENERALIST DEALERS
- VARIETIES OF SHOWS AND FAIRS
- FLEAMARKETS GARAGE AND HOUSE SALES
- ESTATE SALES THRIFT SHOPS
- OTHER SECOND-HAND SOURCES
- MUSEUM SALES SHOWCASE CENTERS
- LIMITED EDITION PROMOTION
- DEPARTMENT STORES
- THE CATALOG TRADE
- MAIL-ORDER CONTACTS

WHERE TO LOOK for and where to find the material with which to form a collection is a fascinating challenge. With the exception of contemporary limited editions, the antiques, art, and collectibles sought by collectors are either in private hands, or already in the channels of the trade. Since the latter includes dealers' stocks, auctions, warehouses, fleamarkets, thrift shops, even pawnshops, and some may still be buried in the earth, or possibly under water, the combinations of chance that lead to an individual collector finding a specific item would seem to pose enormous odds.

❲ "THE TRADE"

What is known as "the trade" is a complex, disorganized international bazaar, made up of large and small establishments, both retail and wholesale, with a mix of scouts, pickers, knockers, and hustlers. It includes the exclusive private dealer and the antiques supermart. It has peculiar business practices, weird and wonderful characters, and merchandise that ranges from worthless to priceless. Each, from the mangiest fleamarket to the sophisticated international auction house, is independent, and yet interconnected. For the most part, matters are arranged for the convenience of the sellers, yet the collector is the ultimate customer who must make sure not to become the ultimate victim.

❲ GOLDEN FLEECE

There are those for whom seeking their treasure is a pursuit of the Golden Fleece—fraught with adventure, and, if successful, crowned with triumph. On the other hand, it may also be compared with looking for a needle in a haystack—that is, painstaking, frustrating, and tiresome. Most collectors see it as the former, and self-congratulation for achievement is seldom as intensely pleasurable as that of a collector in the throes of satisfaction, having made a desirable acquisition. This is often in proportion to the

effort required and the obstacles overcome rather than the merits
of the find itself.

If someday it ever becomes possible to store the description and
whereabouts of every single item available in the collecting market
into a computer, the likelihood is that there would be fewer collectors. The challenge to find the specifically wanted item, to be
always on the lookout, to pry it out of fortune's grasp by being
luckier than others, and more alert, are essential to the whole enterprise. And constantly, the dream that a second-rate example
can be replaced with a splendid, superior, perfect one serves to
motivate as well.

On the surface, it might be assumed that where one hunts
depends on what one has decided to collect. There doesn't seem
to be much point in looking for Victorian hatpins in the shop of a
rare coin dealer, or an Art Deco chess set in a second-hand clothing store, yet they might well be found in such seemingly inappro-
priate places. Because flux—that is, the constant mobility of goods
—characterizes the collecting market, the collector is aiming at
a moving target.

❴ PATTERNS OF DISTRIBUTION

The traffic in the collecting trade circulates in various patterns,
often reversing directions. While some local dealers buy from
wholesalers, others sell to them; often they buy and sell to one another simultaneously. Wholesalers may comb through an area in
trucks, buying for cash and taking immediate delivery of wares the
dealer may have bought privately and finds unsuitable for his or
her trade or has bought especially to turn for a quick profit, or is
simply of interest to the buyer and agreeably priced.

In the book, coin, stamp, and autograph fields, much of this is
done by mail and telephone as well as special catalog and auction, but the process of circulation is the essence of the markets.

A survey of the total collecting territory is best started at the
top and the terrain followed down to the grass-roots level, where
most are involved.

❰ PRIVATE DEALERS

The hierarchy of retail dealers who cater to collectors is usually thought to be headed by those with elegant galleries on smart thoroughfares or nearby side streets, but this is not the case. Private dealers whose premises are not disturbed by shoppers or mere lookers, who see their clients only by appointment, are at the top of the heap. However, any idea that they are too delicately constituted for the rough and tumble of the world of trade and hence keep to an ivory tower is mistaken. These are the shrewdest, toughest, sharpest, and usually most successful, especially in the field of art, but not far behind in the others they penetrate. They cater only to a small segment of collectors; in most cases they do not own large stocks, but they have access to other collectors who wish to sell, dealers in every range below, and the imagination, knowledge, and salesmanship to deal on very high levels. They are on intimate terms with art and antiques experts, the museums for which they also buy and sell, and whenever possible, on a social footing with supercollectors. They are interested only in "the best" and are also considered to be best at intrigue and manipulation.

Certain dealers who do have public shops and galleries place their assistants and clerks between themselves and the general public. Actually, these dealers expect little business to come in "off the street," and count on the staff to handle any that does. However, should a stranger arrive in a Rolls-Royce, it is most likely that the newcomer will be welcomed by the owner or an official of the firm. Books, prints, rare coins, ancient art, and the cream of quality in almost every field of collecting are offered in not necessarily elegant, but somewhat exclusive settings.

❰ PRIVATE CONSULTANTS

Consultants acting in a free-lance capacity may furnish sources for collectors seeking to develop and enrich their collections. Methods of compensation vary from a fixed fee, which may be on a per diem or even per annum basis, or a percentage of the price of the items acquired. Whether they are scholars, museum officials or unattached experts, they are usually well informed as to where fine examples are available, many times in private collections known only to a few. Dealers and auctioneers keep in touch with them, furnishing useful information for locating material and offering private opportunities when they arise.

One of those who set the pattern was the great Wilhelm von Bode, "kaiser" of the pre-World War I Berlin Museum. His was a benign form of blackmail, as it was mutually understood that what Dr. von Bode blessed for the collector was also worthy of going to his museum as a donation or bequest. It was said of von Bode that "He knew where every picture is, where it was before, and who is going to buy it." Since his expertise extended to art objects as well, his figure dominated the art markets of his period.

William Glackens, the artist who was an old friend, set Dr. Albert Barnes on his way to formation of the splendid Barnes Foundation collection. Bernard Berenson built his career on advising Mrs. Isabel Gardner and later the dealer Duveen. More recently, Dr. Sherman Lee, director of the Cleveland Museum, guided John D. Rockefeller III in his search for oriental art. Supercollectors are rarely without professional advisers.

However, individuals in the lower echelons of collecting need not consider themselves barred from consultation with experts. Having ascertained who in a field is knowledgeable, any collector with a bona fide inquiry will find that experts are approachable, often with no fee at all, or in proportion to the circumstances.

(SPECIALIST DEALERS

In every field of collecting a growing number of dealers specializes to some degree; this includes a proportion who confine their interests to particularly narrow channels. For example, while American folk art is considered a specialty, Pennsylvania Dutch or pre-Revolutionary New England folk art defines regional and period outlines followed by some dealers within that specialty. Certain dealers trade only in antique Wedgwood, others in Renaissance bronzes, while ancient near-Eastern coins, Persian carpets, Russian stamps, Georgian silver, or modern graphics hold the exclusive interest of others.

Often such dealers-in-depth are former collectors, occasionally they are scholars in flight from the academic world, and sometimes chance alone explains their exclusivity. This was the case with an individual who, on inheriting a fine collection of Tiffany glass, used it as a nucleus for building a career as a dealer in this rare art glass, happily deserting his former occupation as a display designer.

Since specialist dealers can concentrate on a particular market, seeking the exceptional and the best while in the process developing a clientele to appreciate and pay for it, they usually command choice prices for their wares. However, since such dealers are expected to guarantee the quality and authenticity of their offerings, many collectors believe that even the steepest prices paid to a truly outstanding specialist will eventually turn out to have been worth paying. Since their standards are high, they may sell off less than top quality items as comparative bargains, at least they claim to do so.

([GENERALIST DEALERS

The average generalist dealer is the average collector's most available resource. Unlike the usual status specialist dealer, this one welcomes beginners, and on learning the nature of any collector's wants, will first try to find something of interest in the shop's inventory. Experienced dealers have learned that buying items with a single customer in mind can be a costly mistake, and unless there is a good rapport over a period of time, based on the collector's status as a reliable customer, they are cautious. The need may have been filled, the person may have switched interests, be financially strapped, or simply not like the item. Thus it takes more than a cursory request to incline a dealer to follow up by actually searching for the wanted pieces. However, the collector who develops a dealer's confidence, may sometimes take an unwanted item, thereby securing a most important ally in the formation of a collection. The dealer who actually is happy to add a regular customer will often take the trouble to learn and study the specialty, giving the collector those two heads that are so much better than one.

Many small dealers are dependent on bigger dealers who visit them regularly to buy their outstanding finds. However, the former sometimes resent the condescension of the bigger dealers and prefer to hide away their goodies for their own retail customers. The role of regular client is a good one and worth cultivating.

⟨ VARIETIES OF SHOWS AND FAIRS

Shows, markets, and fairs are not restricted to the collecting trade, but are especially characteristic, because in a field where one-of-a-kind is more the rule than the exception, they greatly increase the chances for buyer and seller to meet. It has been calculated that some sort of antiques, art, or collectible exhibition or sales event is staged on every day of the year. Not only do many dealers close up shop to "make" these shows, but also increasing numbers have found it expeditious to permanently give up their stores and to travel from show to show as a way of life and of business. There are dealer gypsies in every field, with truck and station wagon as caravan.

Shows vary in class and caste. Prestigious both professionally and socially, society-charity-sponsored shows such as the New York Winter Antiques Show and Philadelphia's University Hospital Show are usually "vetted" by their organizers for quality; only well-reputed dealers of status are invited. The invitation itself becomes a form of accreditation. These exclusive shows encourage dealers to bring outstanding material; they "save" for months before a major show. The previews are considered special opportunities for collectors and are used to raise money for the sponsoring group. For many years the London Grosvenor House Antiques Fair, held under the patronage of royalty, has been the prototype.

Although such exclusive shows, with their rarefied atmosphere and high prices on choice specimens may seem to have no meaning for the average collector, the contrary is true. The few dollars' admission is indeed a case of charity beginning at home, because of the opportunity to see, price, inspect, and possibly to handle (if so permitted). Dealers are usually more patient with visitors to shows than with lookers in their shops. Most of the dealers bring what they call "small stuff" to these shows, with less affluent and beginning collectors in mind. Often the dealers will be softer on prices toward the end of a show. In general, they go to shows to make new customers as well as to make sales, just as less prestigious dealers do.

Museum "villages" and historical associations employ such fairs and markets as fund-raising events. The annual Antiques Fair held at the Old Museum Village of Smith's Clove in Monroe, New York, invites dealers who meet the museum's standards. Their booths are arranged around a village green, and Early American crafts are demonstrated in conjunction with antiques, primitive tools, historical Staffordshire, and similarly appropriate material.

Religious nonprofit institutions of all faiths sponsor shows of all descriptions and quality levels. Sometimes the organization's members bring in their personal possessions to sell at a member's booth, creating an even greater mélange of merchandise, inviting to the collector whose time and curiosity encourage browsing in the hope of a lucky hit.

Experienced collectors are somewhat skeptical of businesses that specialize in arranging art and limited-edition shows prepackaged for religious and philanthropic organizations. The sponsor receives a percentage of the sales, but the worthy cause aspects stop there, as the items offered are rarely bargains nor exceptionally enriching to collections.

Commercial fund-raising art and antiques auctions and sales are often run under the auspices of a charity that receives a set percentage of the "take." This permits buyers to make out their checks to the charity in the hope that they can take the amount as a tax deduction. Some organizations actually advertise, "Checks can be made payable to charity."

Purely commercial collecting shows come in all sizes and varieties. One of the largest held in the United States is the National Antiques Show, which attracts over three hundred dealers to an annual convocation in New York City. The merchandise is enormously varied in this type of big show, with coin and stamp representation as well as contemporary miniatures, a range of neo-antiques from iceboxes to vintage electric light bulbs, and authentic classic antiques of every type as well as reproductions. Jewelry is well represented, from inexpensive reproductions to costly, rare antiques.

Also commercial in character, but usually comparatively small, are the "crazy collectible" or nostalgia shows catering to the self-titled nostalgia freaks. They feature advertising collectibles, political Americana, tokens and medals, comic items, post and trade cards, railroadiana, bottles, and toys. One advertises, "comic books, big little books, movie materials, Disney items, science fiction stuff and any nostalgia and memorabilia collectibles." Collectors are invited to "come as anyone you wish, come as your favorite hero, or your favorite foe . . . cash prizes awarded." Thus collecting invades the entertainment area, a continuing trend.

Shows are often held in combination with conventions of specialist organizations, such as stamp, coin, and bottle clubs and associations. The former two arrange themselves under the heading of *bourse*, or exchange, with dealers paying for selling space. Here also specialization plays a part, with subdivisions in the larger shows, or individually small events. Collectors often time their vacations to visit these shows, to browse, buy, sell, and attend specific lectures and seminars.

The crush of people at the opening of every type of show reflects the anxiety of collectors to achieve priority in seeing what is available. Where there is no preview, collectors have been known to volunteer to act as assistants to dealers with whom they have close relations, gladly helping them to unpack and set up their booths, in the hope they will have time to look around and make an early, precious find. Dealers do not confer this favor lightly, since they also use the preopening period to search for what they consider bargains and rarities. This stage of a show is always a hectic one as dealers "deal" under pressure.

⟨ FLEAMARKETS

The fleamarket, once considered a quaint Old World curiosity, has not only come to the New World, but also at times appears to be the most common retail outlet in our economy. Originating in locations where thieves and second-hand dealers congregated on certain days to offer their wares, foreign fleamarkets gained the name when purchasers learned they risked becoming fleabitten on close contact with their bargains, often used clothing. However, those interested in curios and antiques found it worthwhile to risk the fleas, and antique dealers just a cut above second-hand status began to rent stalls, booths or carts, luring dealers as well as eager runners and hardy collectors.

Country dealers could bring their wares for exposure to city dealers and retail buyers, giving them an outlet for quick sales, reinforcing the market as a weekend enterprise. Municipalities traditionally arranged for space on payment of a tax or fee, setting up stands and roofing over squares. In this fashion the Clignancourt market in Paris, the Caledonian, later Bermondsey Market and Portobello in London, and Rastro in Madrid, among those internationally known, were established. Some cities have two classes of fleamarkets. In Brussels the snob market in the Place du Grand Sablon has bright awnings for its stands, while the one in the Place du Jeu de Balle has no such ornamentation for its less distinguished quarters.

After a time, city dealers with regular shops, often in better neighborhoods, would close them on weekends when fleamarkets were most active, and become regular attendants there, bringing suitable items from regular stock and generally raising the standard of merchandise shown. Dealers, decorators, homemakers, and collectors soon frequented such markets, and most importantly, foreign dealers and wholesalers came, each buying at a different price level or discount, with "special" no-discount prices for tourists and sightseers.

When the fleamarket idea took over in the United States it became more of a movable feast. Rather than the reference to a traditional market, as in Europe, it is conferred on any group of sellers of old, second-hand, antique, or new merchandise. Most of them are small and transitory. However, some are large and permanent. For many years the huge weekend fleamarket at Englishtown, Pennsylvania, covering many acres and attracting visitors from many states, advertised, "world's largest fleamarket." Carnival barkers, serious antiques dealers, artists, little old ladies, students, craftspeople, and peddlers set up in business in the ancient tradition of a universal fair. Homemade candles, farm-cured hams, antique furniture, silver, brass, and quilts might be next to dried flowers, vintage automobile parts, imported caftans, and used household goods.

Runners, dealers, and collectors who know enough not to waste time on tacky reproductions vie to look through shoeboxes of odds and ends brought in by neophytes, in the hope of making a lucky find. In the early dawn hours dealers check through each others' stocks, searching for items that will appeal to their trade.

Collectors of offbeat items and neo-antiques are the most likely to be successful at fleamarkets, but others are optimistic too. Since rental fees are low, many private individuals bring their possessions to sell; this has the attraction of being virgin merchandise in the recycling market, hence potentially treasure trove. Scouts, pickers, hustlers, runners, knockers, and higglers who have no settled place of business, who buy bargains for the quick turn to sell to dealers, will cover as many markets as thoroughly as only they can, in a frantic effort to find those "sleepers" hitherto unrecognized.

❲ GARAGE AND HOUSE SALES

House, garage, tag, and barn sales boomed, as products of a do-it-yourself attitude in the early 1960s, when the volume of duplicate and obsolescent household goods and other possessions began piling up faster than the average American home could contain them. Having noted that dealers and auctioneers buying out a household often leave some of their purchases on the premises, marking them with price tags and advertising locally, some individuals decided to follow that example. When they cleaned out attics, cellars, and garages, moved, or for some other reason preferred cash to continued ownership, they held their own sales.

The motive was to get better prices than the low figures offered by dealers and pickers, and before long, aborted collections and unwanted collectibles and antiques were included, adding to the selling appeal. The varying degrees of the owners' ignorance of values made prices uneven, as some items were too high, others too low, but that attracted buyers looking for the latter. Garage and house sales and their variations found a place in the suburban pattern as the country auction and sale had on the earlier American scene. It was even followed, although to a lesser extent, in metropolitan areas where apartment house or supermart billboards were often used for advertising such disposal sales.

Professionally run house sales, where the owner pays a percentage of the total amount taken in to the individual or firm that arranges the sale, by pricing, tagging, running, and advertising it, are usually of more interest to collectors than to dealers. Dealers are looking primarily for bargains in any field, while the collector seeks particular items and is willing to pay more than the dealer.

Obviously, the quality and selection of material required to interest the professional investing effort in such a sale would be more than minimal. However, there is a tendency to "salt" or add commercial merchandise to add volume and interest in these cases. In addition, fakes and reproductions are here sown in fertile soil.

When associations of antiques dealers organized to stop garage and house sales in their cities and states, claiming the loss of sales tax to the community, they were reflecting their own loss of business, both as buyers and sellers, and pique at being shut out. Some solved the problem by joining what they couldn't beat. Some even set up fake garage and house sales, just as they had invaded the fleamarket scene.

(ESTATE SALES

Some house sales are truly "estate" sales in the sense that family members are closing out the households of aged or deceased relatives, and these are especially attractive to collectors. Here, as with all bona fide private sales, they are up against the competition of the professional picker and dealers, who are skillful in grabbing the cream. Seeing them advertised, or otherwise learning of them, those in the trade use all sorts of stratagems to get in before the public, and when they do, leave little of value for others. However, the eager collector can develop countermeasures, and by having a specialty, concentrate on looking for that, without distraction.

Neighbors and friends may have the advantage of advance knowledge of the offerings at such private sales; however, the interior of every home is a mystery to outsiders, and a tantalizing one for collectors.

⟮ THRIFT SHOPS

A truly institutional resource for many collectors is the thrift shop connected with a philanthropy. With the blessing of the Internal Revenue Service, gifts made to charity may become tax deductible. This advantage to the donor brings items of considerable value and collectors' interest to these shops.

Some shops have a large and continuing volume of outstanding material because they have generous donors and a realistic appraisal policy; these become special stops on the collectors' rounds of hunting grounds. However, any charity thrift shop can produce a potential find, and some collectors become addicted, finding it impossible to pass one, fearing to leave a potential treasure undiscovered.

Dealers are regulars at thrift shops, and between their friendly arrangements and personal rapport with management, and volunteers' tendency to grab the worthwhile antiques, art, and collectibles for themselves, it takes a clever and lucky private collector to snatch a treasure. However, many persevere and do so. For the most part, here again the collector of neo-antiques and offbeat original items will fare the best.

⟮ OTHER SECOND-HAND SOURCES

Resale or second-hand shops, sometimes known as private thrift shops, vary from general junk stores to specialized furniture, bric-a-brac, clothing, fur, jewelry, and brass and copper, as well as book stores. They may use the word "thrift" in their business names, but do not have any relationship to philanthropy. However, collectors in many fields consider them important territory in the search for material. As they may buy directly out of a home, the people who run these shops have access to items other than their specialties and often make fortuitous finds. A second-hand silver dealer may pick up a rare antique clock, or a furniture dealer a desirable oriental rug.

House wreckers, junkyards, and ship breakers now advertise directly to private individuals, offering smaller artifacts as well as paneling, fireplaces, and ship wheels. Considered from the viewpoint of contemporary archaeology, they make interesting sources. For many years, Tiffany windows could be found for a few dollars and the trouble to get them; now house wreckers are more likely to set trends than to follow them, but the sheds and acres of plumbing and less prestigious stained glass still bear exploring for adventuresome collectors.

⟨ MUSEUM SALES

Museum shops sometimes sell duplicates or deaccessioned overflow such as pre-Columbian figures, Egyptian scarabs, shards of Greek pottery, and similar items, as well as original graphics, textiles, and contemporary folk art. Authenticated and fairly priced, they may set a neophyte collector on a right path. However, their principal sales are usually of reproductions of antiques and art. The latter would not be recommended as the base for a serious collection, but there are some who believe that the reproductions marked to show their origins may serve as fill-ins until the originals can be acquired. In other instances, modest collections based on these reproductions are formed, and sometimes are germinal to more ambitious, authentic endeavors.

The Smithsonian Institution has ten such shops, divided among its several museums. The Metropolitan Museum of Art in New York City has included a hand-crafted sterling silver parrot, copied from an eighteenth-century sultan's treasure, in the inventory of its reproduction shop. The facsimile copy sells for $1,850, a price said to reflect skillful artistry rather than mere commercial production.

Sophisticated collectors know that museums not only buy from, but also sell to dealers and occasionally auction some of their holdings despite a critical body of opinion that believes that deaccessioning is rarely to the institution's interest. However, the merits of the argument aside, museums do not deal directly with the public in these matters, and as a rule disposal of important holdings is attended with as little publicity as possible. The obvious reason, reticence to discourage gifts that might be withheld if the donor thought they would be marketed has usually turned out to be a sound one.

As a rule, items of interest to collectors that are the property of museums would seem to be forever out of their reach, and usually this is a fair presumption. But there is a remote possibility that a collector interested in some such work might find a dealer in the good graces of that institution who would be in the fortuitous position of making some exchange or other arrangement that by chance would be acceptable. The hope is slim indeed, but some collectors are powerfully persevering. However, it is advisable that all parties to such transactions be prepared to have them revealed without being embarrassed by the disclosure.

(SHOWCASE CENTERS

Showcase centers that are dedicated to the promotion of the arts and crafts of a particular people or culture are usually subsidized by governments and foundations. The Association of American Indian Affairs, and the governments of Ireland, India, Poland, Mexico, and many others exhibit and sell traditional handcrafts and art of their sponsors at permanent galleries, sometimes associated with other national activities, such as tourist development.

The American Indian Arts Center, part of "gallery row" on New York City's Madison Avenue, shows Navaho rugs, Kachinas, Eskimo carvings, silver and turquoise Indian jewelry, carvings, quilts, and baskets. Foreign countries send both antiques and crafts, and collectors of textiles are particularly alert to those from Eastern Europe and India. In some cases, fine arts are also included, and here too collectors find this type of resource to be of interest. Most such centers are located in metropolitan areas, but it is not uncommon to find privately owned craft shops carrying their merchandise throughout the United States.

❲ LIMITED EDITION PROMOTION

The collector of commercial limited editions is usually more sought-after than seeking. Millions of mailing pieces offering subscription opportunities for plates, figures, coins, medals, paperweights, records, prints, posters, and decorative objects of all sorts flood the mailboxes of prospective buyers. Promoters literally bombard the public, automatically conferring the title of collector on hoped-for subscribers.

Observers pronounce the campaigns mounted in behalf of this multimillion-dollar industry to be as inventive, high-powered and high-pressured as any in the realms of advertising and merchandising. A large part comes directly from the manufacturer or mint, some through wholesalers and jobbers, and a portion from the retail stores and mail-order organizations that have committed themselves to orders or that buy the overflow.

Because the so-called secondary market, which was supposed to produce the profit for buyers, was so slow to develop, several firms have created listings, and price guides have been produced. Since these can so easily be manipulated to encourage buyers, they should be checked against the reality. In some cases they may prove somewhat exaggerated on the up side; in many cases they bear no relation to the sad truth that commercial limited editions have generally not born out the optimistic advertising. Bona fide limited editions for which prices rose enormously such as the well-known Doughty birds were comparatively few in number, and the work of considerable artistic merit.

❲ DEPARTMENT STORES

The idea of searching for classic or vintage antiques and other collectibles in a department store seems far-fetched, and indeed it may be for the most part; however, there are department stores throughout the United States, Canada, Great Britain, and Japan where the pleasure of saying "charge it" is added to the joy of

finding an old valentine, rare map, stamp, coin, book, antique silver, china, glass, metal, furniture, or piece of jewelry. Shell and
mineral shops, autograph departments, and art galleries are also
found in such establishments; sometimes they are concessions, in
certain instances the merchandise is merely on consignment, but
they usually have knowledgeable salespeople, and the store itself
is the responsible seller.

When department stores do buy antiques, art, or collectibles for
sale on their own accounts, their practice is to avoid buying from
private persons. They buy from dealers or importers. Occasionally
in the field of crafts they buy privately, but this is the exception.

Department stores have a policy of marking down merchandise
that does not sell after a given period; smart shoppers look for
markdowns, an occasional collector's bonus.

⟨[THE CATALOG TRADE

Book, stamp, and coin dealers practice catalog selling extensively,
as do autograph and print specialists. Some firms and dealers send
out catalogs gratis, others charge for them. Whether published
on a regular basis or sporadically, they are valuable assets to collectors both in finding items for their collections and as value and
price indicators. Auction catalogs may be bought as the occasion
arises or regularly subscribed for. At least one important international auction firm includes a service to alert subscribers to items
of special interest as they come on the market under its hammer.
This too is a form of mail-order collecting for those who take advantage of it.

Shortly after the Metropolitan Museum of Art acquired the
million-dollar Greek krater that crowned its collection of ancient
Greek pottery, a Dallas department store catalog made almost as
many headlines. The Neiman-Marcus Christmas offering of a pair
of "genuine Greek bellkraters . . . unearthed in Southern Italy
dating from the 4th century B.C.," at a price of five thousand dollars, astonished all but those who have seen rare coins, stamps,
and manuscripts at higher prices in catalogs with much smaller
circulation!

(MAIL-ORDER CONTACTS

A great deal of collecting is done by mail, largely in answer to advertisements placed in collectors' periodicals, either describing the material in sufficient detail or sparking additional correspondence. At some levels, lists and snapshots can be had without charge or for small sums, giving the buyer a more detailed description and consequent assurance.

Experiences run the gamut from disastrous to highly satisfactory. Problems in dealing with private individuals usually arise from poor packing and consequent breakage in transit or lack of complete description. Not all transactions with the most reputable dealers are concluded without problems either, but the advantages of the wider potential of mail-order buying cannot be overlooked in many fields. Prepurchase correspondence is the recommended course, clarifying such matters as condition, insurance, packing care, and costs. In some cases, haste in reply may be essential to secure the item; only the collector knows if the risk is worth taking.

It is as possible to be a valued mail-order client as a shop or gallery regular, and many collectors have never met the sources of some of their most desirable acquisitions.

CHAPTER 7

AUCTIONS AND OFFBEAT SOURCES

OF ALL SOURCES for collectors' acquisitions, none have the excitement, drama, intensity, or potential for success or failure presented by a bona fide auction.

Unfortunately, the increasing popularity of auctiongoing as a diversion has increased the number of phony sales. However, since these rarely if ever have any material the serious collector seeks, those so credulous as to be taken in by them will probably continue to pay a high price for their entertainment. There are enough problems and pitfalls for collectors in bona fide auctions to warrant concern, but the first and primary problem is the discovery of material suitable for a particular collection. How to learn which sales are taking place and what they are offering require a degree of organization, whether for the international, national, or local auction scene.

❲ CATALOG QUEST FOR ACQUISITIONS

Perhaps the largest scope is the simplest. Supercollectors and dealers subscribe to the important sales catalogs at the beginning of each auction season. This is done from lists that may offer as many as twenty-five different *series* of auction catalogs from a single firm. Depending on the number of categories and the sales in each category, the cost might be fifty dollars for the Americana series or several hundred dollars if paintings, furnishings, silver, oriental art, antiquities, and other categories were included. Air mail and international mailings are proportionately higher, and it is not difficult to envision international art collectors laying out large sums to be alerted in plenty of time to consider making a trip to view a potential acquisition and possibly arranging for an expert to give an opinion on it.

Collectors and dealers on that level simply open the daily mail and are thus informed. Should the chore of going through so many catalogs seem overwhelming to them, certain auctioneers offer an additional service for those seeking *specific* items, advising them when such will be coming up for sale.

So much for the heady heights of international collecting. Less ambitious or amply funded collectors may, by following a few leading domestic publications, be well posted in advance of auctions of importance that will be advertised in sufficient detail for determination as to the advisability of buying a catalog by mail. Coin, stamp, book, autograph, and print collectors are among those who soon learn which firms hold regular auctions, and there is hardly an interest, from Americana to oriental art, that cannot be followed by seasonal or single subscription to catalogs.

Collectors who cannot go to the preview of a cataloged sale may write to the auctioneer for further details on a particular lot, and upon deciding to bid, can place the bid by mail or by telephone after having made the necessary arrangements to establish identity and credit. Certain catalogs are richly illustrated (these are the more expensive ones), but in any case, not every lot will be photographed. It is just as well to be sure of the wanted item before bidding blindly in absentia.

While every bona fide auction is advertised somewhere, not every one of them is cataloged, and many catalogs are numbered lot listings rather than full descriptions. Most of such sales of interest to the majority of collectors will be mixed rather than specialist sales. Even at established auctions, mixed sales, with decorative furnishings taking the lead, are the most plentiful. These may consist of items from private homes, individual collections, lots belonging to the auctioneer (having been purchased especially for the auction), or lots from dealers' stocks—in short, a mélange of what the auctioneer believes is salable. To be on top of these requires that the collector be on friendly terms with the auctioneer, who knowing what the collector seeks, will either respond to inquiry or sound an alert by post card or telephone. Local auctioneers do this for the dealers who are their regular bidders, and will do the same for collectors who establish a firm relationship as a good client.

❲ NOT ALL "BIG TIME"

While the excitement of huge sums bid for individual pieces makes for headlines, these transactions are a very small portion of total sales, even in the elite auction houses where they take place.

At the same time that a hammer goes down on some highly publicized purchase, many "gones" are uttered throughout the land for "lot consisting of box of miscellaneous items," often thrilling collectors who thus acquire some much-wanted and long-sought, if not costly piece.

The authentic local estate sale that occurs when the household broken up is large enough to warrant such an event, or when several are combined for the purpose of an auction, has been and continues to be the grass-roots base for collecting. Testifying that "You can't take it with you," such sales sadden collectors with chill thoughts of mortality while heartening them with the vision of exciting finds. In addition to clues from the auctioneer, collectors know that they must themselves search out the odds and ends, going through boxes and barrels, using great care to thoroughly cover the auction room for possibilities.

Whether a great collection or an old household, the auction is a form of recycling that appeals to the gambling instinct in all collectors.

❮ BEATING THE BUSHES

Hunting for antiques, art, and collectibles in the established channels of the trade occupies the majority, but increasing numbers of collectors are developing skills in locating material through more unusual, creative approaches. Requiring a more aggressive attitude and a greater output of physical energy, they take collecting out of the semisedentary activities sphere to become competitive with tennis or golf, if not mountain climbing.

Not all of the more dynamic endeavors meet the purest ethical standards. Many of the endeavors simply adapted from those developed by dealers do not necessarily indicate duplicity, but show no special sign of integrity, either. On the other hand, digging bottles out of a public dump makes no demand on the most fastidious morality, though the physically fastidious may resist.

The lengths to which collectors will go to beat the bushes includes acting as volunteers for philanthropic fund-raising projects in order to get into private homes. They also offer their services at church bazaars, rummage sales, and charity auctions to be on hand to spot, sequester, and often buy at minimal prices when valuable items are processed. Their presence as volunteer workers in thrift shops has been noted, often in competition with dealers.

When offering to buy privately they may use the old trick of offering to pay a great deal more than a comparatively worthless item's value, at the same time slipping by "something else" of great value as trivial. This is in the tradition of the English higgler (something between a peddler and a knocker) who bought a peasant's rickety pigsty to get a Roman silver bowl used for throwing slops to the swine.

Aggressive collectors can also be persuasive. The great English painter Turner, who hated to sell a picture, was once greeted by a collector who said lightly, "I have some pictures for you in my pocket," while showing a fistful of currency. Turner answered, "You seem like a sensible fellow," and sold him one. Like the great dealers, great collectors know the right approach to use when confronted with an opportunity.

(EARLY IN THE MOURNING

When a fox hunter is "in at the death" it is the end of a hunt; when a collector reads obituary notices the hope is for the start of one, namely advance news that a collection may be going to enter the recycling process. Dealers, auctioneers, and museum officials also bestir themselves at this point if not beforehand when potential material surfaces in connection with illness, old age, or death. News of divorce or serious business reverses also alerts what have unkindly been called "the vultures."

Extreme tact may be used if approaches to the mourning family are required; it is not unusual for friends of the deceased, fellow collectors, to offer to aid the widow in disposing of a collection. Such helpful advisers have been known to improve their own collections rather than the lot of widows and orphans. In the case of husbands who preferred to keep their wives in ignorance of their expenditures on collections of coins, stamps, or books, unconscionable "friends" have kept widows in continued ignorance, much to their cost.

❲ CLUBBY PERSUASION

Novice members who enter collecting clubs and associations with exceptional rarities, coveted by their fellows, can be offered swaps and deals that leave them with a larger but poorer selection. Except for this caveat of "new members beware," the growing number of clubs and collecting associations provide valuable contacts, comparison, and exchange of information among collectors. This information will seldom if ever include sharing private sources, as collectors prefer to keep competitors in the dark in this regard.

When an association or club is formed in a new collecting specialty, it is considered a sure sign that the organizers have exploited their easy finds and are less paranoid about discovery of their sources. Even close personal friends who are collectors do not share certain intimate details of collecting transactions. Two great autograph enthusiasts, Dr. Thomas Addis Emmet and Theodorus Bailey Myers, whose friendship rivaled that of Damon and Pythias, made a conscious decision not to specialize in conflicting categories. Thus they were able to supply each other with tips, even exchange material, but did not put their friendship to the ultimate test of collectors' rivalry.

❲ LEGAL LIQUIDATION

Lawyers who would resist any connection with ambulance chasing as abhorrent and unprofessional are not above using their connections for the formation of their collections. Like bankers, lawyers sometimes get an inside track through the settlement of estates in which collections are involved. The decisions as to how, where, and through whom collections are to be liquidated are usually made by executors and trustees, who need not be actually dishonest to manipulate matters so they get a crack at desirable antiques, art, or collectibles. Should they manipulate in such a fashion as to get them for little or nothing, that *is* dishonest, and occasionally such matters come to light.

Most estate collection transactions are probably legally correct, but occasionally lawsuits indicate that someone believes that profitable hanky-panky has taken place, usually through the connivance of dealers, as alleged in the famous Rothko inheritance case, but sometimes private collectors get this sort of an inside track unassisted.

❲ ILL-GOTTEN TREASURE

Although insurance companies seem to prefer silence to publicity and are said to pay ransom where necessary, the question of how much stolen art, antiques, and collectibles is recovered leads to another—namely, how the missing material enters the market. It is generally believed to be bought by fences who pass it into the trade, but there are said to be private collectors who could resist the offer, "Wanna buy a watch?" on a street corner, but might not pass up a clock, painting, graphic, rare coin or stamp, vintage gun, or some other desirable addition to their collections. They might only suspect it to be stolen, but would not pursue the matter too closely.

One envisions the frustration of a collector with a cache of stolen masterpieces or masterworks, forever doomed to enjoy them in eerie solitude. Of course, not all stolen items are unique, and positive identification of much that is antique might be difficult if not impossible. A spate of advertisements in the collecting press describing stolen items and offering rewards indicates belief that the point of a first sale is the best hope of recovery.

All through the ages soldiers have been great "liberators" of collectors' treasure, and war-torn countries are tragic sources for succeeding collectors. In addition to tomb burials, archaeologists find that valuables buried for temporary safety from pillage are the second greatest source of treasure hoards as they turn up centuries later.

Not all the towels marked "The Plaza," the napkins saying "Harry's Bar," or the ashtrays spelling out "Ritz" have been lifted by light-fingered guests. These and others like them can be purchased in specialty and department stores by people who are forming collections of items purporting to have been "taken" in

the course of travel. This type of souvenir acquisition, which includes napkins, coasters, matches, china, silver, and glass from restaurants and hotels, is supposed to reflect a certain pride of
achievement at having pulled off a succession of minor larcenies,
and although considered gauche by the sophisticated, it has a considerable following.

Among groups known for sticky fingers are "biblioklepts."
When they borrow books that fit into their collections, they may
intend to return them, but somehow forget. In the words of
Samuel Pepys, whose own love for books led to problems with his
admiralty expense account, they are not "punctual returners."

Some famous collectors of the past who would absentmindedly
drop expensive bibelots in their pockets and leave a shop without
paying, might find the bill upon arriving home. In the same tradition, although even more immediately, some restaurateurs put the
price for the "lifted" tableware on the bill with the food and
wine.

⟨ DIGGING IT UP

A plague of collectors has been responsible for illegally digging
fossilized animals and plants out of the public lands in the American West. Scientists complain that private collectors digging for
themselves, and dealers who sell this material, loot the national
heritage while obliterating important scientific information. The
mass merchandising of fossils as curios, art objects, as decorative
materials, and as jewelry became a multimillion-dollar business.
Fish and bird skeletons millions of years old have been listed in
internationally distributed catalogs and sold to Europe, Japan,
and Australia, without any records of spot or strata from which
they came, destroying scientific efforts to gain more knowledge of
the evolutionary process. Collectors are said to leave orders for
rarities with dealers, further encouraging the destructive trend.

Not only scientific but also archaeological and artistic problems
of authenticating material taken out of its context have existed for
centuries, as graves, tombs, and other finds have been robbed in
order to sell the material for profit, often directly to collectors,

usually to dealers, and indirectly to museums. Pre-Columbian, Greek, Scythian, Chinese, and Indian materials are from among the countless cultures so pillaged.

An interesting and adroit solution to illegal digging for ancient treasure has been reported from Germany. In the area around Cologne, a trading hub for thousands of years, the valley of the Rhine is so rich in Roman and Celtic artifacts, often found in tombs, that amateur illegal diggers were bypassing scholars, finding treasures and selling them directly to private collectors. As the professionals from the Cologne Museum realized that they were missing out on spectacular and important finds, it was decided to offer the amateurs a pact. This would permit them to dig under the supervision of museum staff, and when the finds were registered, and if necessary restored by the museum, the amateurs had the option of keeping them for their own lifetimes or selling them to the museum at negotiated market prices. In any case, the museum and the finder could both be satisfied, and it appears the new approach has gained the interest of other institutions.

The struggle of the collector for and against illegal traffic has international ramifications. Some say that all antiquities are a form of loot anyway; others believe it is time to advance beyond that attitude. As governments now position themselves for protection of their antiquities, there are still many skeptics, but it is believed that some progress toward attribution will be made in this fashion, by treaties restricting both inflow and outflow.

([CREATIVE CONTACTS

Striving young artists and craftspeople, still struggling for recognition, give prescient collectors their most rewarding opportunity to build worthwhile collections. Sometimes the collectors are equally young and comparatively impecunious, and if they both gain success with maturity, the satisfactions for such a collector are doubly gratifying.

Another aspect of art and craft acquisition involves no purchase, but rather an exchange of services, permitting the creatively endowed to pay their bills with their work. So Watteau exchanged a painting for a wig, and many a doctor and dentist has become a collector in exchanging health for beauty.

Artists who inscribe their works as gifts seem reconciled that the recipients are likely to sell them, aware that should the former become famous, the value of the latter will increase. With a view to the future as well as the past, autograph collectors write to prominent people in such a fashion as to evoke a reply, enriching their collections by an inadvertent gift.

In general, artists are more likely to exchange work than to buy one another's; however, to be an artist is to have a special appreciation for, as well as access to art, and some have formed fine collections by a combination of purchase and exchange. Art critics have formed collections of gifts of art works, thereafter extolling the artist and raising the value of their own collections.

⟨ PATRONAGE

As an alternative to exchanging services, becoming critics, wives, lovers, or friends of artists, collectors can acquire their work by commissioning, thus becoming patrons in a grand tradition. Not only painting and sculpture, but also silver, ceramics, glass, jewelry, tapestries, and quilts are among the works that are especially created for individual collectors.

Famous artists of our time are less likely than Raphael or Rubens to accept commissions detailing the subject, size, and colors, but as we know, they did not always satisfy their patrons either. However, commissions for special projects are accepted by artists of lesser to greater stature, and in many cases, are especially sought.

By acquiring commissioned works, the collector makes a creative contribution, at the same time adding something absolutely unique to the collection, certainly the most limited of all editions.

⟨ PRIVATE NETWORKS

Not only the superrich can have private, if not secret, agents to search for and to alert them when an item for the collection becomes available. Although most collectors either regretfully rule out such seemingly impossible dreams or do not even entertain them at all, quite a few modest but enterprising collectors would appear to be oblivious to limitations. They successfully recruit their own private networks of agents to help them run down their trophies.

Imbued with do-it-yourself doctrine, they usually begin with their immediate families, although willing aunts, uncles, and cousins are recruited and trained as well. The collector who specializes can alert these along with friends and fellow workers to focus on reporting on a limited field for a start, personally following up each trail. If warranted, finders' fees prove most efficient rewards.

General social situations and relationships are deftly milked as collectors find opportunity for inquiry. Some collectors are aware that they bring up the object of their search with obsessive tenacity, but prefer to be considered bores so long as they are successful collectors.

New, crazy, nostalgia, and vintage collectibles are some of the designations that nascent fields are given both by their condescending critics and their loyal adherents, the latter group consisting of a growing body of specialists who seek their prizes by dint of arduous legwork.

Although advertising materials, pioneer electronics, industrial and mass-production prototypes, toys, comic books, movies, sheet music, records, and that vast panorama that goes under the heading of trivia have become stock in trade for dealers, many collectors in these fields are resourceful, imaginative, and creative, making it a combined hobby and sport to form their collections by pursuing them into the cracks and crevices of industry.

They watch for bankruptcy proceedings, read trade journals for news of old firms that are moving or going out of business. They develop ingratiating techniques to persuade people to let them look through stockrooms, warehouses, barns, and storage areas. In general, they are indefatigable, passing up no opportunity, no matter how remote the chance of reward might seem. They truly invest themselves in collecting.

❪ SKILLFUL SEARCH

In the past, collecting was associated with leisurely browsing. Only dealers were thorough in terms of making their rounds with speed and efficiency. Quickly yet completely scanning a household, basement, attic, stockroom, or show booth without overlooking material of interest is not a mere convenience, but also an important business asset.

Most collectors never developed such skills; only a few did. A new generation of collectors, imbued with the ingenuity to blaze new trails, the energy to pursue them, and a greater sense of urgency about the value of time, is more concerned with proficiency in covering collectors' territory.

The specialist collector has an immediate advantage, having the necessity to focus intensively on a limited material, subject, or form. In many instances, such items have already been segregated from the rest. If not, the trick is to look at everything, but "see" or appraise and evaluate only that of concern. Attention is held only by what is being sought, be it cut glass, silver, copper, or brass, specific kinds of porcelain or pottery. The eye scans the entire shelf but stops to concentrate only when attention is demanded; otherwise it discards without absorbing.

The collector whose scope is wider searches best by subdividing space into graphs. Walls, counters, cabinets, even ceilings and floors are mentally blocked into individual territories, each one explored from left to right or top to bottom, or possibly in reverse, but always in a habitual order. Should the collector's attention be diverted, as often happens, the eye returns to that spot, so that nothing is ever passed over without having been evaluated or sequestered for further consideration.

In addition to marking off an area as if it were a graph, the veteran takes note of drawers, boxes, enclosures, and closets, making sure to exploit every opportunity of the terrain, inquiring for specific items that may not appear to the roving eye, or perhaps are in transit, but available.

After a certain amount of experience, the collector's eye develops a laser beam that cuts past masses of inventory to penetrate what is consequential. Knowledge accrues, and judgments are made more accurately and swiftly.

Although the collector with a specialty can search more efficiently than the browsing general collector, there is a point where some of the pleasure of leisurely browsing is lost, and the specialist who too completely blocks out everything but the single obsession does limit his or her vision in a larger sense.

⟨ COVERING SHOWS EFFICIENTLY

Collectors visiting shows and exhibitions, many of them with hundreds of dealers and displays, can literally become dizzy unless they plot a strategy, using the program or floor plan. One system is to check off the exhibits that are known to be of interest from previous experience, or have come to the visitor's attention as worthwhile, outlining a route and sticking to it. If further visits are possible, this is done on the first visit and a leisurely stroll taken through the show or exhibition on the second or later ones, getting an over-all view of what is offered as well as bringing new dealers into consideration. If only one visit is on the agenda, the first course is followed on arrival and the second thereafter, unless the definite stops are so few as to be easily incorporated into the total coverage.

In general, it is better to carefully examine fewer units than to take a cursory glance at many, although the very skillful veteran may risk the latter under the pressure of time.

Collectors do not like to alert dealers they do not know about their area of specialty until the entire offering has been visually explored. At that time, if nothing has surfaced, it is considered "safe" to ask, and if as an additional bonus, the dealer may suggest sources that do have what is wanted, the collector, however wary, is gratified.

⟨ THE TOURING COLLECTOR

In the United States, antiques collectors on tour can consult Mastai's, a directory of dealers that lists them according to their specialties. There are also local associations that offer maps to encourage and assist travelers who are prospective customers. The temptation to look is always great, although there are certain objective criteria to serve as guideposts. The chances of finding a Pennsylvania Dutch *Fraktur* in a New Orleans shop committed to elegant French decoratives would be slim. However, there is another school of thought maintaining that the best place to look for bargains is in the shop whose owner wouldn't be interested in having an item in the first place and would be delighted to get rid of it in the second.

Although there is something to be said for seeking collectibles in unlikely areas, this is largely a matter of hoping to find them at low prices, rather than in a large and choice selection. In reverse, where an item is highly valued, it will usually be presented in goodly array, although priced accordingly.

CHAPTER 8

UNDERSTANDING PRICES AND VALUES

WHILE SOME MAY dream of unlimited funds with which to buy whatever they please for their collections, paying any price, most dream of finding their long-sought treasures for little or nothing. And you can't tell by the dream who is rich and who is poor, because no collector ever feels rich enough, and the wealthiest drive the hardest bargains. Price is not established in the checkbook nor the price guide, but in the value judgment of the collector.

The vocabulary of collectors and dealers gives some insight into standards of value and clues to their responses and reactions. The phrase "I bought it right" translates that the buyer thought the price was on the low side. "I paid too much for it" implies that the price was more than the buyer wanted to pay, but not more than the item was worth. The inference is that one might always do either better or worse; there is nothing to indicate the perfect equilibrium of a "fair" price. "It was a steal" describes a very great bargain, and "It was robbery" is usually sighed by one who has paid a high, possibly exorbitant price for an item deeply desired.

Whatever the level of a collector's finances or budget, every transaction represents a struggle between fear of being "robbed" and a desire for possession. Some have a taste for this contention and a talent for winning. They develop techniques suitable to the source, be it thrift shop or international auction room.

(PRICE FANTASY AND FACT

Price structure in the collecting world has been likened to that of commodity, securities, and similar exchange markets, but it differs, being less orderly and much more fragmented, with each transaction being absolutely unique. Lack of production cost figures results in antiques, art, and collectibles having an individually judged value index intrinsic to each piece. The price depends on where, when, and from whom it is bought. As each object surfaces on the market, the price changes from what the original seller receives to what the buyer-collector pays. It may be increased many times, depending on whether it went through the hands of one or more knockers, runners, scouts, and dealers on the way to its owner on a particular cycle. The path may take it from garage sale to second-hand store to fleamarket to dealer, auction, and finally collector. It may go from attic to knocker to wholesale exporter to importer, jobber, dealer, and auction before landing in a collection.

Obviously, from the collector's viewpoint, the ideal purchase is at a primary stage on the ascent from the original source to the later destination. It is only at this level that a "steal" is likely. On the other hand, there is a point at which movement from hand to hand no longer justifies increased price, and if the item doesn't stop there, it is going to warrant a claim of "robbery" when the collector who finds it and can't live without it protestingly makes the purchase.

(PRICING IN PRACTICE

Although every item will not be unique in the world, there is enough variation, be it in condition, signature, or markings, to warrant individual calculation of price. As each goes into the merchandising mill, someone passes judgment on its worth in the hope that the next buyer will concur and pay the price now asked.

Thus the runner who finds what he believes to be a first-rate antique quilt at a garage sale or thrift shop for $35 may get $50 the same day from the wholesaler who stakes him, and who in turn offers it to his first dealer-customer the next morning for $150, but accepts the proffered $100. This dealer then takes it to a big antiques show, pricing the quilt at $250. A folk-art specialist dealer sees it while it is being unpacked, and recognizing it as outstanding, dickers with the dealer, ultimately paying $200. At this point the scenario may take several turns. The rarity and quality of the quilt may prompt the dealer-expert to price it at $1,000, in the belief that it is a masterpiece and that eventually a museum or collector will pay accordingly. However, if the piece is merely an unusual example, the price tag will probably be about $400, and there is a probability a collector may get it for $350.

On the other hand, should the runner have brought in an ordinary quilt for which he paid $20, the wholesaler for whom he works as a sharecropper may take it for $25, selling it the next day for $40 to a dealer who eventually sells it for $75 to a customer furnishing a country house.

The multiplicity of possibilities that result from the fact that each transaction is unique requires that the collector establish a strong base for determining prices, subject to the needs of the collection and founded in the realities of the marketplace. This latter necessitates an understanding of how dealers relate to one another as well as to private collectors.

❪ DEALERS' WHOLESALE VS. COLLECTORS' RETAIL

The antiques wholesaler, preferring to do business on a massive scale and therefore with dealers who must sell at retail, often tags the merchandise at the potential retail price level determined by his experience, using it as the figure from which to quote the dealer's discount price. There is nothing sacred about that retail or list price—it is as much a psychological selling tool as any "manufacturer's list price" and as the object goes into the stream of distribution, the list price usually gets lost except as a flexible basis for mark-up. Actually, every dealer buys at a price that allows for a margin of profit when the item is sold. Like any other merchant, the dealer in antiques, art, or collectibles includes rent, light, heat, telephone, insurance, interest on loans, transportation, advertising, packing, shipping costs, and salaries when computing business expenses. Not all dealers develop prosperous operations; some barely scratch out a living, others fail entirely. All must buy selectively to remain in business, as the collector discovers when selling possessions and sadly finds out just how sharp a buyer the dealer can be.

Although the markets for rare coins, stamps, books, autographs, and manuscripts are subject to the same economic mechanics, dealers in these specialties, which depend on the expert's guarantee, issue catalogs and price quotations to collectors that do not exactly coincide with market actuality, but vary, usually on the high side. However, when dealers buy, supply and demand take over, and if they expect to have to hold the items for long, they will completely ignore the prices they are asking for similar items, offering very little or entirely rejecting such objects.

❡ GALLERY AND STUDIO PRICES

Craftspeople and artists are charged one-third to one-half commission by galleries and dealers who handle their work, often by exclusive contract. Sometimes if they are dissatisfied with the income thus received, artists and artisans will sell sub rosa directly to collectors at prices lower than what their representatives are asking, chancing the cancellation of the contract by a wrathful dealer. Art collectors have been known to acquire the works of young comers in this fashion, promising to help their careers by their patronage.

Not all who enter the artist's studio dicker successfully. The collector who isn't hard-nosed may be at a guilty disadvantage in the presence of talent and make an unwanted acquisition, being embarrassed to buy nothing or offer too little directly to the creator. And the artist who has just spent the money you paid for a painting on rent or groceries can't return it should you change your mind. The gallery will allow you to take art on approval, without recriminations if returned in a reasonable timespan.

❡ LIMITED EDITIONS

Struggling to raise sales in a declining automobile market, the Ford Motor Company briefly advertised one of its models on television as a "limited edition," and why not, when salt and pepper sets are similarly described?

The commercial abuse of the phrase that originally referred to books, especially published in quality, therefore costly editions, that had to be limited in number because there was a limited market, and that were collected by book lovers, has made it almost meaningless. Yet truly limited editions of anything very fine, made for connoisseurs willing to pay for quality, will always have a place with collectors. Actually, they need not be so described, since they always come in prestated small quantities and become more valuable without promotion, but merely by virtue of their excellence.

⟨ UNLIMITED EDITIONS

A totally different framework programs the pricing of commercial limited editions of plates, medallions, figures, and certain graphics as well as other items. Seemingly simpler than the twisting channels of antiques, art, and other collectibles distribution and pricing, it is at least as tricky, and needs explanation if the collector is not to be a gullible victim.

A veteran observer has pronounced the promotion advertising campaigns and sales efforts in this field of collecting to be the most inventive, high-powered, and high-pressured in all merchandising and advertising, and full-page advertisements in newspapers and magazines attest to its cost.

Yet the most fascinating aspect of "limited edition" promotions is that most of them do not tell the size of the edition! The reason for that is simple: The manufacturer does not know what it will be when advertising it, since it will be as large as the number of orders received. Thus, the most important aspect, comparative rarity, cannot be equated in the price. The limitation is not number, but time—the quantity of orders that can be taken in the period given—incidentally, a period that has been extended and renewed in many cases, when the orders did not achieve the manufacturer's idea of a satisfactory profit.

The initial production cost, like that of other manufactured items, is computed to include basic material and labor, plus packaging, promotion, and advertising. Whether or not the manufacturer or mint is selling the commercial limited edition directly to the collector, or to a wholesaler, jobber, or retailer, the collector pays for the promotion. This additional part of the price adds nothing to the worth of the items at the time of original sale, or at any later time.

One importer of a limited edition line of plates indignantly and publicly severed relations with jobbers and retailers, claiming their exorbitant prices to collectors tripled and quadrupled those he was charging at wholesale. He was especially embarrassed because they were all advertising different prices at once, and some collectors were getting suspicious and backing away from the items.

Lack of a secondary market on which to check claims of high prices for commercial limited-edition collectibles has added to the skepticism of many observers. In an effort to counteract this, some promoters set up "market quotations," but they turned out to be little more than self-serving price guides without statistical authority, leaving the collector to the mercy of supply and demand when money actually changes hands as the collector decides to make a "secondary sale."

([EVALUATING PRICE GUIDES

These so-called price guides for plates and other limited-edition items joined the long lists of publications purporting to quote "average" prices on antiques, art, and collectibles from Victorian settees, eighteenth-century paintings, and vintage typewriters to Avon bottles, political buttons and badges, hatpins, dolls, guns, music boxes, and player pianos, to mention a few of the items in countless guides produced privately and by well-known publishing houses.

The most successful few appear in new editions annually, proclaiming their dates. Many others try to bury the publication date, so they will appear to be current. Since time is of the essence in quoting price, the outdated guide is essentially useless.

Some price guides are illustrated. These range from unidentifiable to fair to good. Those with many listings usually rely only on brief descriptions that are weak and inconclusive, where one-of-a-kind dominates and condition is all.

It is generally agreed by knowledgeable collectors that price guides have been responsible for some escalation of prices, are often fictitious, and are of more value to the seller than the buyer. A disclaimer of responsibility, usually in small print, is the most valid information in many of them. Since dealers are notoriously secretive about the prices they actually get, the so-called average prices are arrived at from advertisements and auctions. Where the information originated, what the prices stand for, and how they are weighted would determine the validity of the statistic. Indexes from distorted facts can only induce buyers to pay more than they otherwise would. The price guide as a self-fulfilling prophecy makes the collector a victim and causes one to wonder what the prophet has to gain.

"Who wrote the price guide?" is not a question that can be answered merely by naming the author. The connection of that individual to the trade, whether in the role of a dealer or a collector about to become a dealer, would be pertinent in evaluating its integrity. A bias in favor of inflating the market value of a category can actually push it up, creating widespread acceptance of those hiked-up prices, which will soon be quoted by dealers as "average."

Writing to a collectors' weekly newspaper, an inquirer says he has a cast-iron figure as pictured on a certain page of an antiques price guide. "I have been told the price is a mistake in the book and that this item is worth (a) one hundredth of the stated price, (b) the value is double that stated." The writer wishes to know what to believe.

One can only marvel that the questioner is willing to accept either of such a wide-ranging set of possibilities, and the need to trust a listing rather than one's own judgment, observation, and experience indicates the kind of credulity upon which price guides feed.

How then, with price guides unreliable, prices so various, unrelated to original cost, fluctuating with time, place, and person, does the collector arrive at a decision of what to pay for a given object?

Fortunately, while prices follow the state of the economy, both buyers' and sellers' skills at bargaining, and all the uncertainties of the recycling syndrome, the object itself is a repository of value, and the components of that value, varying for individuals, determine its worth by a scale of measurements offering guidance, if not precision.

A price value equation for almost any collectible can be derived by balancing the twelve following factors. They are not equally important and vary with the category or object for rank and weight. They do work by a sort of synergy. When they are all present in strength, the item takes on a charisma that is reflected in the prices it fetches.

⟮ PRIME CONDITION PRIMES PRICES

Not only the perfection of condition, but also the lack of repair and restoration contribute to value. The closer the piece to its original state, the more desirable it is. A hairline crack in porcelain, flaked-off paint on a toy train, or slight signs of wear on a coin may reduce the value by half or more. It is mint or proof condition that has the bloom of value.

The worn state of most antique tapestries and the permanent loss of color through fading are among the factors responsible for a neglect of tapestries by many collectors. However, a set of Gobelins panels fetched almost $200,000 in 1969, as much for its exceptionally fine condition with brilliant coloring as for its other virtues.

Only in cases of great rarity is imperfection acceptable, and even then it detracts from price.

For most items, poor repair and restoration will decrease the value of an item to less than it would be were the flaw unconcealed.

⟮ THE RARITY FACTOR

You may have the only brown paper bag in the world with your child's first crayon drawing, but he had better grow up to be a great artist before you consider it a valuable collectible. Rarity increases value only when there are other values. In addition, it is comparative. Not only how many exist, but also how many are available on the market make a difference. Also, it is important to know whether the rarity is artificial or contrived. Like diamonds held by a monopoly, art may be held by dealers who release works gradually, to keep the market up, as in the case of the movie studio controlling Disney originals, which dole out their items.

The only known signed Capodimonte figure by Giuseppe Gricci brought $27,600. One unsigned, but known to have been modeled by this master, fetched $15,000. At the same time in the same auc-

tion a similar Capodimonte group, also circa 1750, could bring
only $625, having neither claim to rarity made by the other two!

⟦ CONTENT CONSIDERATIONS

There is said to be a hierarchy of values for different subjects according to the category collected, and while there is some truth in
this, it is one in a constant state of flux.

For years it was said that paintings of anonymous, disagreeable-
looking individuals by unknown artists had little appeal, hence
small value. Yet many portraits that fit this description are now
highly prized and astronomically priced as American folk art.

Gory subjects, whether religious or profane, have long been considered poor value risks in the world of fine art, but the racks of
bloody meat painted by Chaim Soutine rank among the most important paintings of this century, say some contemporary critics,
and great collectors hunger to acquire them.

Within each collecting specialty, certain subject matter is especially desirable for its rarity, historical interest, or relation to its
maker's best period. This is a component of its value that super-
sedes other aspects of subject, whether integral or ornamental,
and requires an appreciation that each collector must develop in a
specific field.

However, especially in the field of antiques, art, and decorative
objects, there seems to be an overriding appeal in gay, colorful,
and upbeat subjects that makes them easier to sell and hence is
reflected in the price.

⟦ WHAT'S IN A NAME?

An old-time country auctioneer boasts that he could always get
more for a "genuine John Smith" painting than one bid for as
"artist anonymous," and there is no doubt but that names of any
sort do impress the naïve. In general, well-known names strongly
attributed bring better prices at auction shops and galleries. However, sophisticated collectors pay only for names that have prestige
in a specialty. Such names may be of the artist, designer, or manu-

facturer, of the original or subsequent owners, but they relate directly to the item. Having been part of a famous connoisseur's collection adds luster to an object because the individual was an expert or was advised by one.

An Art Deco chair may be appealing, but the Cobra chair known to have been designed by Carlo Bugatti has brought $10,000, so highly thought of is his work and hence his name. Two names are better than one, and three even better than two, as in the case of a set design by the Norwegian Edvard Munch for his compatriot Ibsen's *Ghosts*. The fact that it had been in the collection of Max Reinhardt added just enough appeal to raise the price it fetched to $42,000.

Whether Lettie Lane paper dolls, Mettlach steins, Leica cameras, Faberge jewelry, or Rookwood pottery, names that command the respect of collectors will represent value in the price.

Having made the connection with the name, the certainty with which it can be established is another value factor. Clear marks, authentic signatures, and labels, together with bills, receipts, catalogs, and proof of pedigree and origin provide security for which buyers are willing to pay.

⟮ OVER TWENTY-ONE

Like rarity, age must be combined with other values to be of consequence in determining price. Otherwise how would a two-thousand-year-old Roman equivalent of a Colonial copper penny sell for a few dollars, while the Early American coin can bring in thousands of dollars?

Despite its other virtues, and it has many, an Elizabethan silver compote fetched $50,400 because of its age. And $115,200 for the eighth-century vellum manuscript *Sermons of St. Augustine* is a tribute to its exceptionally early date.

It has been pointed out that very often an object survives to become an antique because it is extraordinary and thus has been accorded special care. Thus, "It isn't an antique because it is old, it is old because it had the potential for becoming an antique."

❰ TRULY TREASURED

If only because they were costly, silver, gold, precious and semiprecious stones, ivory, enamels, rare woods, and silks have stimulated artisans through the ages to extend themselves in skill and craftsmanship. The results have intrigued collectors who can afford some of the most expensive treasures available.

Not only gold snuffboxes and silver tureens, silk carpets, ivory jewel cases and royal crowns, but also French eighteenth-century kingwood consoles with ormolu mounts belong to this category. And when gold, silver, and precious stones are high on the contemporary commodity market, their values as antiques, objects of art, and collectibles are further enhanced, although that is not the sole standard of their worth.

At the Lopez-Willshaw sale of precious objects, mostly of the late Renaissance, a total of $892,080 was paid for only thirty objects. Cups of crystal, smoky quartz, and heliotrope were sold at prices between $13,000 and $40,500, and a gold box brought $42,500. At another sale, an eighteenth-century table desk brought over $400,000, overshadowing most jewels, but actually in itself a jewel of precious materials and workmanship.

❰ SCARCE SKILLS

Although the workman may be long gone, the fact that the workmanship is no longer available makes it especially cherished. Obsolescent and "lost" techniques are much sought by collectors and enter into the value considerations of any object.

Guns, armor, watches, tapestries, lacquer, lace, enamels, needlework, musical toys, instruments, rugs, inlaid furniture, and both glass and porcelains of the sort that could no longer be made have a special value that is reflected in price.

A pair of Italian flintlock holster pistols, chased in high relief with figures from classical mythology, so exquisitely constructed that only one screw is visible, were considered a bargain at $14,400.

⟪ CHOICE STYLING

Some styles are also survivors, usually because they continue to assert themselves as exceptional against earlier and later forms. Not everything wins the accolade of time, but that which does keeps a high price as a mark of its high profile in the market.

The Edwardian automobile, Early American highboy, Gothic linenfold panel, and Shang bronze are being accompanied into classical territory by Art Nouveau and Art Deco examples. Despite the efforts of dealers and collectors to establish Victorian design and styling, it still hasn't made it into this august company. A style must be accepted as more than merely characteristic to be considered a value factor.

⟪ ENDORSED BY HISTORY

Historical commemorations bring a wave of rising prices, especially for book, manuscript, autograph, coin, and stamp collectors. Also looking backward, furniture, decorative accessories, costumes, and jewelry related to a period or a historical character follow the general trend and reflect that in the price.

A new school of collectors looks into the future to find souvenirs of events and of political and public figures presently only slightly distinguished but readily available, which they believe will become valuable with the turn of events to come.

It was reported that Republicans especially snapped up a series of one hundred-edition lithographs simulating stamps, satirically depicting Nixon and other leading figures in the impeachment proceedings. They were thought to be adding to their political historical collections with an eye to rounding them out. Nixon supporters who had kept memorabilia of his campaigns were hopeful that their letdown would be somewhat assuaged by some future increase in value.

⟮ THE BEAUTY EQUATION

If, indeed, beauty can be priced and valued, it must be defined, and since it changes with the object, the individual's response, and the specific standards of the moment in any category, the equations vary greatly.

Harmony of form, contrast, scale, elegance, or simplicity of design, appeal of color and texture as well as of material and technique evoke aesthetic appreciation in fine art, and when related to function, in objects of utility as well.

However, there are many fields of collecting in which the uninitiate is at a loss to understand the standards by which connoisseurs proclaim beauty. The dark, mottled Whieldon pitcher, the homely, garish Staffordshire figure, the absolutely plain Queen Anne tea caddy, and the early mason jar are only appreciated as beautiful by those who know what they are and how they relate to others of their kind.

In addition, the element of demand adds an invisible aura that many call beauty on the theory that handsome is as handsome does in the marketplace. Yet the collector who falls in love with what others call an ugly duckling may find that with the passing of time, and changing appeals, it may turn into a lovely, egg-laying, golden goose!

⟮ WHEN SMALL IS BIG

Traditionally, in times of economic and political upheaval, small, precious antiques and collectibles, such as gold snuffboxes, miniatures of ivory, precious stone carvings, rare coins and stamps and jewels, units of great value in small size, known as "transportables," will bring even better prices than the general market reflects. This is value appreciated by those who prefer some portion of their holdings in readily hidden and mobile wealth, impervious to inflation's erosion and, in some cases, to the bite of taxation. Thus, mobility as a value factor can be reduced to a question of compression of much into little, and when this can be accomplished by forming a collection that can fit into a suitcase, the price of such objects rise.

Another and perennial appeal is that of the miniature for its own qualities and as a tour de force, whether as a netsuke or chandelier for a doll house. Finally, the problems of storing large and oversize objects when space is a costly luxury, enlarges the demand for the small and compact.

Yet there are values for bulk as well, especially when within manageable proportions for the private collector. The largest teapot, doorstop, ivory fan, or Indian basket will, if it has other desirable features, have incremental value and price. Truly large-scale antiques are sought by private museums, and for restaurants and commercial display, where high prices paid can be readily recouped by their owners.

(TIMING IS MONEY

Prices may be raised to coincide with exhibitions, articles, books, auction sales, even items planted in gossip columns and collectors' periodicals by promoters of new trends in collecting antiques or art. Collectors who follow fashion and speculative tendencies are the most susceptible to being manipulated; those dealer-collectors who create trends usually have the best collections for the least money and ride the wave as interest and demand develop.

Pop art, especially in multiples, Carnival and Depression glass, and Disneyana have exhibited typical symptoms of the syndrome that welcomes new categories well promoted. When a price quoted for a Snow White radio is five hundred dollars, when two hundred thousand copies of a book on the art of Walt Disney sell for forty-five dollars each, to be followed by a paperback sale of half a million, somebody is doing something right at the right time.

CHAPTER 9

HOW TO BUY, BID, AND BARGAIN

FIFTY SUGGESTIONS FOR IMPROVING COLLECTORS' TECHNIQUES

PRICE IS a measure of value at a certain time and place, hardly the only true test of value, as is sometimes implied. The prices of antiques, works of art, or collectibles of any sort are so flexible that individuals forming collections soon learn that they must develop bargaining skills in order to cope with the practices of a trade that has over the centuries developed an arsenal of techniques designed to maximize its profits.

Less co-operative than dealers, who though cannily competitive, often organize in transient buying and selling combinations as well as in auction rings, private collectors are more often lone victims than lone wolves. There is little sharing of trading experience among them and no common body of accumulated bargaining skills. Each starts out equipped with whatever shrewdness can be mustered and embarks on a painstaking and costly process of self-education hoping, to co-ordinate business acumen with expertise in a field of collecting.

Bargaining is not necessarily haggling, although that too may be required as collectors learn to buy and sell defensively, recognizing that asking prices are perhaps nothing more than a tentative trial, learning to probe and eventually to manipulate as they gain assurance.

Auction bidding is another area where insiders have an edge. Here too the private collector can be victimized both as a buyer and a seller, unless alert to the complex of possibilities. Awareness and experience save many a collector from losing a wanted item, or unnecessarily overpaying for it if won. They also protect against acquiring items that have to be culled at a loss. There's more to that than not scratching one's head by mistake during an auction's progress.

❴ FIFTY SUGGESTIONS FOR IMPROVING COLLECTORS' TECHNIQUES

Before you ask for a price quotation from a dealer, determine the maximum you will pay, having considered your budget and the value elements.

Don't ask for too many prices before getting to the item that really interests you.

Don't let the shabbiness of a place make you feel certain that it is full of bargains.

Be extra wary of a dealer who claims to be taking a loss on every item—if you believe that you are a likely victim.

When you are told the prices of "everything" collectible is up, be ready with your own battery of stories.

Mention the 1794 silver dollar bought for $127,500 in 1974 that could not bring $75,000 at another auction only six months later.

If possible, buy some inconsiderable item for the marked price. Pay cash. Now you are a customer.

Should the item you are negotiating for really have some defect, point it out. If not, do not downgrade unless the dealer makes extravagant claims.

Establish that you are knowledgeable, but without ostentation. Don't "educate" the dealer unless you are old friends.

Don't be backward about naming a figure considerably lower than the one you are willing to pay. Leave yourself some leeway on the up side.

Turn a glassy eye on price guides. Anything in print is already out of date. Besides, the dealer's brother may have written it.

Talk in low tones when negotiating; a dealer hates to have others overhear bargaining procedures.

If the item is consigned, don't hesitate to make an offer and ask the dealer to contact the owner with it.

Don't swap with a dealer unless you are prepared to trade your item in at wholesale and take the other at retail, thus losing at both ends.

Don't be afraid to indicate you like an item, but you needn't say how intensely you want it.

Make your counteroffer firmly. Indicate you are serious.

Mention that you have an alternate choice in mind should this transaction not work out.

For a costly item you want, but can't pay for at once, suggest credit terms, but do this *after* you have settled the price.

Dealers usually want cash before going on a trip; this is a good time to come in with an offer on items that you know have been in stock for some time.

January is an off month except at winter resorts, and dealers may soften prices for cash offers.

If you are interested in limited editions at less than offering prices, look for the closeouts offered in collectors' publications.

On occasions when prices are so firm that you can't budge them downward, you can still demand a discount for cash.

A famous English collector says he once got a discount in London merely for not being an American. (Always try anywhere.)

Many American collectors, suspecting they are buying at a disadvantage when abroad, take on protective coloring.

When asked if they are dealers—and if knowledgeable this often happens—collectors will never entirely disclaim it, hoping to get the trade price.

Some private collectors, wishing to avoid sales taxes and wanting trade prices, establish themselves with a retail registration number and a business card.

On finding a price quoted too high, you may express dismay or disappointment; desist from hostility—it is self-defeating.

Don't hesitate to tell a dealer that you have only so much to spend for a specific item.

Do not tell a dealer how much you have to spend and then ask for an item to fit the price. Dealers are always suggesting this as a procedure. It is good for them, not you.

If the stock is unmarked and the dealer looks you over while deciding on the price, you had better look elsewhere.

Pay no attention to the high-pressure sales pitch. You really don't care who admired it, wants to buy it, or never saw a better one.

Don't tell dealers what you gave away or sold; they couldn't care less, and it marks you as an amateur.

If you offer far too little, the dealer will probably not continue to negotiate. Keep your offers at a realistic level.

Read auction catalogs carefully, including terms of sale—the auctioneer means them.

Introduce yourself to the auctioneer and arrange for checking privileges if you are not a regular attendant at the establishment.

It is advisable to become a "regular" at a superior type of auction rather than to wander about in questionable fringe areas.

Get to know the auctioneer's staff. An occasional tip will be appreciated and possibly reciprocated when information is required by you.

Unless you are a prominent collector, don't worry about secret codes. Just make a clear signal when you bid.

Note whether a lot is by the piece, pair, or dozen.

Sit at the back of an auction in a reputable firm. They won't switch lots or numbers, and you can watch competitive bidding.

At a questionable auction, or where the reputation is unknown to you, be near enough to see that the item you are bidding on is the one you saw exhibited.

Time spent at the presale exhibition is the best investment you can make at any auction sale.

Don't be guided by either admiring or adverse viewers' comments on the items at auction exhibition. The owner may be touting prices up, or a hopeful buyer may be trying to discourage others from bidding.

Never bid on items you have not inspected.

Let the bidding start before you join in. Some don't participate until the first few bids have been made.

Stick with the regular increase if it is moving briskly; try to cut it if the action is slow but stubborn.

Auction prices are believed to average between wholesale and retail, but each winning bid reflects a particular circumstance that may never be duplicated again.

Never forget that the owner may be bidding against you, and in some cases the auctioneer owns the merchandise.

Dealers often form a ring, bidding as a unit to avoid competition among themselves. They later hold a private auction, sharing the difference in price.

Don't hesitate to ask for the source of an opposing bid if you are suspicious of its origin or even of its existence.

CHAPTER **10**

ONLY THE POOR NEED NOT INVEST

COLLECTORS ARE constantly being admonished to rise above crass considerations of money, and rather than buy for speculation or with an eye to investment, to form their collections solely on the basis of their own tastes and inclinations. This good and laudable advice cannot be faulted. The problem is that neither the rich, the well-to-do, or those in modest circumstances feel they can afford to take it. Ironically, only the poor, in their customary right to sleep under bridges, are free to collect without financial considerations. There are penalties for possession.

It was not always thus. Treasures of beauty and rarity have traditionally been amassed by the wealthy for security, certainly with the hope, even expectations of escalating value, but for centuries the collector of art, antiquities, or curiosities was a person of wealth, part of whose holdings could be allowed to lie financially fallow, that is, without providing income or producing profits.

❪ THE GOOD OLD WAYS

The collection recompensed its owner in many ways. It offered satisfactions of beauty, status, possibly hopes of immortality. It represented an expenditure that enriched and embellished the current life style, simultaneously serving as dormant assets. Collections were sold when tastes changed or when, in most cases, traumatic events such as death, debts, reverses, and economic or political upheavals dictated. Normally, until the middle of the twentieth century, collections were considered static wealth, a fine thing to have and enjoy.

Even the money-minded tycoons of the early twentieth century, for whom money structured and defined almost everything, adhered to this outlook. Despite the fact that making money was of paramount interest, often attended with genius, the Fricks, Folgers, Rockefellers, Morgans, Wideners, Mellons, Hearsts, Havemeyers, Huntingtons, and many others like them who lavished millions from their astronomical profits on their collections, never sought to make money as collectors. A spirited duel with a dealer over price was never precluded, but for the most part the collectors were willing to pay well for the best.

At the same time, many not wealthy, but "comfortably off," formed their less-costly collections without considerations of profit, acquiring art, books, coins, antiques, and art objects at whatever rate they could afford. In the early twentieth century, those with advanced tastes and modest incomes could, like the siblings Michael and Gertrude Stein, buy pictures by Picasso, Cézanne, Bracque, and Matisse simply because they liked them. Until World War II, the growing middle class and professionals in Europe and the United States brought forth new generations of collectors who were aware they were accumulating value, a possible form of additional security, but were not concerned with collecting directly for monetary gain. A few exceptions turned collector-dealer.

(SPECULATIVE COLLECTING BOOMS

Collecting for profit as a speculative activity received widespread public attention in the late 1950s when, during a sharp drop in the stock market, an economic analyst noted that record prices at auction were making headlines. He computed the proportionate price rise for antique English silver, eighteenth-century French furniture, and French Impressionist paintings, comparing it with the showing of the stock market, which had made spectacular gains in the previous decade. The art and antiques had by far exceeded the gains of the securities markets. Astute dealers in the collecting trade had already called this to the attention of their customers, but it had not made the financial news before. Many were impressed and entered the art and antiques market as investors, in some cases consulting dealers as they would stockbrokers or financial counselors. Art, antiques, and collectibles investment publications, tip sheets, and so-called experts were soon riding the wave of speculative interest.

("GUARANTEED" PROFITS

Freely quoted assurances of 20 to 50 per cent advances to be made in a few months became commonplace when the market was advancing, subsided somewhat in recessions, but surfaced again at the least sign of a turnaround. The art market was the first to be so involved, but oriental rugs, weathervanes, dolls, Early American furniture, and even tobacco canisters are quoted in this fashion.

Where originally, only well-to-do and wealthy individuals were tempted by the opportunity to profit by speculating in high-quality art, antiques, and other collectibles, those on lower economic levels were also attracted to acquire in such categories as bottles, toys, comic books, and post cards. Blue-collar workers joined the collecting-for-profit boom, and all watched prices go up in the price guides, at auctions, and in advertisements, if not always when they sold under pressure.

A nationwide keeping up with collectomania brought corporations to the art dealers where overflowing corporate cash swelled sales until Knoedler noted publicly that corporations' purchases had become the source of the bulk of that firm's business. The prestige of galleried offices and corridors attracted the Chase Manhattan Bank, which led with over $3.3 million in twentieth-century art, Westinghouse, U. S. Steel, IBM, and many other giants. Some sent their collections "on the road" as visiting exhibitions, some kept them intact, and many also traded, buying and selling.

⟨ INTERNATIONAL COLLECTING
CONGLOMERATES

The advent of big business into collecting for investment and speculation brought other types of international investment corporations to the scene. Their purpose was not merely to buy, hold, and eventually sell art and antiques, or act as conventional dealers, but principally to maneuver financially in the collecting market. Some folded quickly, a few survived. One boasted Swiss banks as well as industrialists among its backers, according to reports. Its activities included control of art galleries around the world. Its "portfolio" varied, at one time consisting of 25 per cent in Cubist and post-Cubist works; between 20 and 25 per cent in Surrealism; about 5 per cent in Impressionism; about 12 per cent in Expressionism, and the balance in contempory art. One firm has published graphic editions and a Dali tapestry, the latter in an edition of 500, at $1,500 each, and a limited edition of 99 sets of 12-place silver flatware in especially sculptured boxes was commissioned. Also a corporate investment project was a surrealist bed and screen arrangement designed by Max Ernst in a multiple edition of 99 at $35,000 each. One of these was purchased for the Admiral House, the Washington vice presidential official residence, by Vice President and collector Nelson Rockefeller. As an interesting footnote, the gallery that sold it to him was reported to have done so at a price below the originally asked $35,000, "after negotiations."

Also structured as a corporation for the purpose of paying dividends to stockholders, and backed by a European bank, is an "art investment banking firm" described by its managing directors as "a system . . . of individual dealers who buy and sell in loose collaborative arrangements." It has a socially and financially prestigious board of directors, and a professional advisory board made up of critics, art experts, and university scholars of importance and influence. Diversified, its holdings include antiquities, antiques including old silver, old masters, and modern art. The New York *Times* reported that this firm's London old master expert found a Giovanni di Paolo "Baptism of St. John" at a Paris auction for $42,000, which was then resold to Norton Simon at $475,000. When a director of the firm notes, "The affiliation not only gives us financial strength but also information and access to a network of expertise," the conglomerate nature of the enterprise seems clear.

("SADISTIC" PRICES

A consumer publication headlined the news that "Nazi Relics Sell at Sadistic Prices," advising collectors to "liquidate horizontally and specialize vertically," so that "if you are into helmets, you won't become sidetracked by Iron Crosses." Despite what was called a murky economic outlook, it was suggested that Nazi relics would appreciate from 15 to 25 per cent each year.

In the climate of "everybody's doing it," a self-confirming prophecy seemed to be taking place on an international level. Those looking for value and worth in the object itself were looked upon as gullible and naïve, as short-term investment potential invaded the thinking of collectors, seeping down to flea-markets and erupting into the mass merchandising of "limited

edition" plates, medals, and graphics in seemingly endless pro-
fusion.

New entrants were added in every field of collecting, to become
envious as well as encouraged onlookers at the spectacle of a New
York dealer-collector's sale of a Jackson Pollack painting for which
the dealer-collector had paid $32,000 in 1956, for $2,000,000 to an
Australian museum in 1973. A continuing series of farewell viewing parties and tearful interviews by the newly bereft owner kept
the story in the headlines and public consciousness, raising cynical
eyebrows, but pleasing dealers in every field of collecting who consider such coups splendid propaganda for business.

⟨ CULLING FOR REFINED PROFITS

Even more fascinating to an art world divided between horror and
admiration was the spectacle provided when Norton Simon
"refined" his collection of great masterpieces by selling what many
deemed to be its crowning glory, a Cézanne still life. The price of
$1.4 million was said to reflect an irresistible profit, although most
critics agreed with Lord Clark, who found it incomprehensible
that a man who claimed to love art "and could certainly afford to
keep the greatest painting in his collection . . ." would sell it.
Soon after, Simon's purchases of Asian art were stepped up, in
one case leading to a dispute with the government of India over
the ownership of a tenth-century bronze temple sculpture for
which Simon had paid $1 million. Business analysts noted that
the auction sales over a period of three years in which Simon
disposed of $15 million in art indicated that there were possible
advantageous tax considerations that might explain the buying
and selling as purely financial transactions, moving assets among
corporations, foundations, and various personal and family funds.

⟨ THE MIDAS TOUCH

Satirists chortled that it had come to such a pass that even the
wealthiest could hardly afford the pleasure of collecting for pleasure. By paying high prices and selling at higher prices, they created

a situation in which most had to safeguard their treasure unseen and unenjoyed in vaults, and like Midas, ruined all with the golden touch.

Some thought that the United States tax law permitting deductions to the donor at the rate of the market value of the item at the time of the gift had encouraged museums to help collectors and dealers establish astronomical price values to be translated into generous gifts to institutions, these actually at the expense of the average taxpayer, who has to make up the difference to the treasury.

In some quarters of the world collecting scene it was believed that fear of inflation was largely responsible for the zooming price spiral of some antiques, art, and other collectibles; even the employees' pension fund of the nationalized British railway system bought works of art for the purpose of hedging against inflation.

❲ SUPERCOLLECTOR TECHNIQUES

Whatever the causes or even the consequences, the supercollector's speculative market fascinates the less affluent millions who comprise the majority of collectors. They marvel, slightly envious, wondering why even proportionately scaled minor successes seem so evasive. However, in examining the operations of the money-making supercollectors as individuals or corporations, it becomes apparent that they do more than make fortuitous choices in selecting items for their collections, or even in buying low and selling high. They operate with a different set of goals than the individual who is interested in forming a collection, and by a different set of standards as well as methods. They are actually in the business of collecting money, not art, antiques, books, coins, or stamps; the objects are simply a form of exchange.

The subject of the collection is chosen only for its potentially increasing value.

Given sums are invested and reasonably quick returns expected on the part assigned for short-term gains.

Backing is available for additional outstanding opportunities should they arise.

The collection is not kept intact over a long period; turnover and exchange are required for money manipulation.

Objects are sometimes bought in one currency and sold in another to "launder" corporate money.

Objects may be admired, but everything is essentially merchandise to its owners.

Experts are preferably on staff to keep confidentiality.

Corporations or foundations are usually set up, even for a private supercollector.

Objects are moved from one to another of the above, for tax advantages.

Transportation of objects from one country to another is also a commonplace for tax and corporate advantages.

Tax and legal advice come from sources skilled especially in dealing with investment and speculative collecting.

Critical and scholarly connections are essential to establish authenticity. Money is spent freely on research.

Critical and scholarly connections are also important. In reviews and articles, they may tout what they have privately advised purchasing.

Some prices and values are established solely for gift and tax-deduction purposes. This can be done by exchanges without any money involved.

If losses are taken, they are kept quiet, leaving the reputation for success intact.

⟨ IMPROVING YOUR ODDS

Although not in the class of speculative supercollectors financially, nor possessed with their goals of profit, the more modestly funded need not give up the intention of increasing their financial security, as a by-product, if not as the principal purpose of creating a collection.

Perhaps all collectors who do not consider their purchases as expenditures for transient pleasure, as they do for costs of golf, travel, theater, or concerts, are savers, investors, and even speculators. By holding some of their assets in the form of collectibles, they count, hope, or gamble on their marking time, keeping up with or outstripping the general position of the economy. In the opinion of most economists, the odds are with them if the collection qualifies according to basic value guides. The better the collection, the better its growth potential. However, there are considerations of outlook and approach to the financial aspects of collecting that improve those odds.

Anyone contemplating the formation of a collection, or the possession of one, should consider how much of total net worth, and what proportion of income to designate as available for this purpose. Occasional buying binges, stretched credit, and struggles between budget and desire are commonplaces for most collectors. However, the individual who does not keep a reasonable relationship between reach and grasp destroys pleasure and peace of mind and distorts the scope of the collection as well.

An objective view of the collection from a financial perspective allows the collector to outline an intelligent balance, appraising the role of the collection in the total budget. It also provides the means with which to enlarge and advance the quality of the collection and helps increase its value as saving, investment, and speculation, but within prudent goals.

Collectors who consider the following questions will find that their answers (or lack of them) will present a self-portrait and possibly an indication of the prudent and practical measures that lead to better control of the financial elements involved in forming a collection.

What percentage of your total assets can you afford to hold as a collection?

Have you reckoned the cost to you of your collection? Do you include interest loss on the principal?

Do you value your collection annually?

Do you know the current replacement price?

If you had to sell, what would it bring? Is it easy to liquidate?

Do you calculate your annual collecting expenses such as insurance, repairs, travel costs?

Do you set a fixed figure for acquisitions for your collection in your annual, monthly, or weekly budget?

Would you consider borrowing from a bank to make an advantageous purchase?

If you borrowed money to make a purchase, would you return it before buying again?

Do you know where to go for a reliable, objective appraisal?

In what circumstances would you want the appraisal quoted at retail or in wholesale valuations?

Can you calculate whether your collection's market value has kept up, exceeded, or fallen behind the rate of inflation?

Have you considered reducing your cash tax payments by making tax-deductible gifts of items from your collection to suitable recipients?

Are you aware that the present market price and not your cost determines the extent of the tax deduction?

Do you sometimes make a purchase not required for your own collection because you know you can sell it profitably?

Do you just keep and store less desirable items, or do you sell them and use the money to acquire superior examples?

If your spouse or heirs had to liquidate your collection in event of your incapacity or death, have you left instructions?

Have you figured the addition to your estate made by the value of your collection and the consequent tax burden?

Have you discussed this with your accountant or attorney?

CHAPTER **11**

PROFILE OF THE COLLECTOR

- ACQUISITIVE
- INQUISITIVE
- QUALITY-CONSCIOUS
- JUDGMENT
- TRADING SKILLS
- SENSITIVITY
- COLLECTOR'S EYE
- TASTE
- EMOTIONAL INVOLVEMENT
- PURPOSEFUL
- PERSISTENT
- AND A LITTLE BIT OF LUCK

DEALERS SEE collectors primarily as buyers, also as potential sources. Auctioneers see them as bidders, consignees, and eventually, obituary notices. Curators and museum directors view them longingly and sometimes sadly as donors; sociologists, as status or image seekers; and psychologists as studies in sublimation.

In searching their memoirs and biographies, and examining their collections to discover the characteristics that distinguish outstanding figures in their creative roles as collectors, it is obvious they come in all shapes, sizes, and sexes. Among them are introverts and extroverts, the fine and ignoble, misers and spendthrifts. To present the aspects of their variety might be interesting but hardly useful in this connection, since it is the qualities they share that delineate the profiles of individuals who form exceptional collections.

These characteristic traits are not shared in equal measure; in each case the emphasis differs. However, all successful collectors have them all to some degree; possibly the most successful include more of them in greatest measure.

([ACQUISITIVE

A strong thrust of "I want it" precedes the formation of a collection. People who merely admire, wish for, think about, or hope for one, lack the drive necessary to create and develop the reality.

Obviously, economic means play a part in costly collections, but plenty of rich people do not collect, and the acquisitive individual may take something originally very low in price, such as Depression glass, barbed wire, or fruit labels, even cost-free graffiti, to form an outstanding collection.

Not all who are acquisitive amass what may be deemed collectible objects. Some show a preference for gold bullion, clothing, real estate, or companies with which to form conglomerates. Others secure caches of worthless refuse. The much-publicized Collier brothers, who crammed their New York City brownstone residence with tons of junk, illustrate the result of this impulse gone awry. If you are acquisitive you may not become a collector, but you won't become a collector unless you are.

E. G. Langui, the Belgian scholar, likens the collector to Don Juan in his possessive instincts, finding that he "forgets all the trials it cost him and sets out in pursuit of his next prize."

The great collector Gulbenkian lived the last fifteen years of his life in comparative simplicity in hotel rooms in Portugal, continuing to buy at an accelerated pace the fabulous works of art that he sent to his magnificent house in Paris. He could live without his possessions, but not without acquiring more of them!

Pleading "a psychological defect," a hitherto respectable figure who had been caught with several specimens, admitted his enthusiasm for collecting minerals had turned into a compulsion to steal. Such kleptocollectors, whose acquisitive urge outruns the capacity to pay or to find their treasures in the marketplace, are sorry examples who win a certain degree of sympathy from their fellows who manage to keep similar passions under control.

(INQUISITIVE

Not all who are acquisitive are inquisitive; it takes a combination of the two to shape the profile of a successful collector. Not merely a willingness, but also an urge to trace the origins, dates, makers, history, or whatever else may be pertinent to evaluating, appreciating, literally "knowing" the object is the mark of a successful collector at every level. This starts with intensive scrutiny of the object itself and by following the trail of the technique, the biography of an artist, the dates of the merging of workshops or factories, patent records, the geography of a region, or sometimes the mythology of a culture; it ends as true possession. Otherwise ownership may simply be a form of rape in which the piece is superficially "taken."

If necessary, wealthy collectors employ experts and scholars to furnish them with the information they may not have the time or skill to procure themselves, but if they are truly creative collectors, will themselves participate in the detective work that goes under the dignified and formal headings of research and study.

A strong strain of curiosity is indispensable in the makeup of a real collector, not only in the desire to know everything possible about each item, but also in the process of acquisition itself. "Have you ever seen another like this? Which auction? Do you know who bought it? Can you remember the approximate date?" The more successful the collector, the greater the number of questions.

(QUALITY-CONSCIOUS

Nothing separates the casual dabbler from the real collector more than respect and desire for quality. Lord Clark, who as Kenneth Clark was director of the London National Gallery, speaking critically of recent profit-motivated collectors, was asked how they differ from their predecessors, the tycoons of the turn of the century. He answered that those early tycoons were "all working to get the best."

The search for quality by those with top financial resources might seem normal to average folk who presume it would be a natural concomitant of wealth. Yet financial magnates, concerned with profit appreciation of their holdings, often buy with fashion and quick salability in mind, overlooking the aspects of inherent quality. When an art collection was donated to a museum by a well-known Wall Street figure, it was noted that while there were plenty of great names, not a single first-quality work was included. It was called a large group of small-scale works of secondary importance.

The hallmark of a serious collector is adherence to quality standards, and it unites collectors of teddy bears, bottle labels, pincushions, and art of whatever period. Since quality is a confluence of condition, workmanship, pedigree, attribution, material, subject, and design, it requires that an object have the virtues needed to distinguish it from the run of the mill.

Having initially succumbed to temptation by accepting a somewhat attractive specimen with shortcomings that are not too obvious, the true collector will overcome it, to eventually sell or trade the item. Capacity to cull remorselessly is what forces the growth of a quality collection.

⟪ JUDGMENT

A capacity for consideration of many factors, and ability to form a conclusion in a reasonable interval, are characteristics of most successful individuals and special traits of the ideal collector. Indecision and resultant inaction can't create collections, and typically, failed collectors tend to speak of their "almosts and nearlies."

Facility in making judgments gains respect, brings dealers to collectors with desirable finds, and by the very exercise of decision develops confidence and superior discrimination. It is not necessary to make mistakes to learn from them, but only the decisive individual, willing to make judgments, gets the opportunity to learn from experience.

Not only the objects themselves must be judged, but also circumstances in which they are offered and the prices to be paid. A sound scale of values in the general affairs of life contributes to good judgments made in the course of forming a collection. A dealer's reputation, the trustworthiness of a new source, even the value of a man's word must often be taken into account.

⟪ TRADING SKILLS

A healthy delight in a good buy makes all collectors kin, but successful ones seem especially good at bargaining. The good trader surfaces at the highest levels; history indicates that aristocratic collectors such as Charles I, Catherine the Great, and any number of Popes excelled at getting the most for their money.

That is the point, because buying cheap is not the same as buying well. The desirability of the item is its primary appeal; after that is established, paying the lowest possible price becomes a challenge.

J. P. Morgan's complaint that the most expensive words he ever heard were *unique au mond*, indicates that though he spent millions of dollars on his fabulous collections, he was never quite resigned when he had to meet what he thought was an exorbitant price, even for the only and presumably best of its kind in the world.

The collector's anxiety to acquire certain items in forming a collection makes him or her especially vulnerable, but clever collectors make every effort to disguise this, developing techniques and tricks, mostly after the fashion learned from dealers who exercise them on collectors when buying from them.

(SENSITIVITY

"How can anyone so crass, coarse, vulgar, and common be an art collector?" is a question that has been asked many times. Although this phenomenon has been noted over and over again in the two thousand years since the observation was first made in ancient Rome, both sophisticated and simple folk continue to reiterate the query.

The fact that a similar question is often asked about artists affords the answer. Social polish, fine or even merely good manners, and delicacy of feeling are simply not involved in an individual's creativity as artist, craftsman, or collector. Collectors need only the sensitivity to appreciate whatever they collect—having that capacity, it can be turned into a skill.

The collector may seem insensitive to sentiment, decency, honesty, and affection, but will be sensitive to the delicate "oil spot" on oriental porcelain, the "shadows" in old Waterford glass, or the intricacy of a wood carving. Uneducated, uncultivated, offensive in manner, shrewish, aggressive, or petty, the ceramic collector has the important sensitivity to reject the lifeless perfection of a machine-made pot that cannot be compared to the lively curve of a handmade model.

Many a collection testifies to the finesse of a boor. The ideal collector may or may not have a sensitive soul, but does have sensitive responses to objects.

(COLLECTOR'S EYE

The ability to spot an item of value and interest in unaccustomed surroundings and unusual circumstances is somewhat misunderstood, but nonetheless a splendid asset that is shared by all capable collectors.

Often mentioned, rarely described, it is presumed to be based on a sort of extrasensory perception with which some are mysteriously gifted. Even experts speak of it with some awe, usually in condescending connection with fine collections formed by business or lay persons without their advice.

In fact, there are fortunate individuals whose visual perception happens to be natively sharp and who are exceptionally good at retaining visual information, as some are with written or oral information; some are well endowed to retain all three. Should they be exposed to many examples, alert to the distinctions among them, inquisitive, acquisitive, and inclined to form a collection, these will develop what is known as the "collector's eye." In general, alert individuals with good visual perception add a valuable ability to the list of those characteristics that form a skilled collector. The "instinct" to spot antiques, art, or collectibles is nothing more than that.

What seems to be a mysterious gift is actually the co-ordination of information that an individual may have subconsciously gathered, usually leading to apt conclusions.

❲ TASTE

Another myth, that it takes innate "good taste" to form a successful collection, also needs to be explored and exploded. There is no such thing as good or bad taste; to have taste merely means that one can differentiate and be selective. The old warhorse "I only know what I like," which is also used in a defensive manner in other fields of collecting besides art, can be translated freely as "I have no taste." Cynics agree that the individual who knows only "what I like" knows nothing of interest to anyone else.

Taste is not a vague intangible; it *is* knowing what you like, but above all, *why* you like it. Successful collectors can explain the reason for their preferences.

Any particular style in art, decoration, clothing, literature, or music may appeal to a collector and be considered worthy of collecting, or it may be a fusion of several, creating a new perspective. Great collections can be formed in the conventional taste, following the generally accepted standards of the past or present; they can also be selections of the unpopular, unusual, hitherto considered ugly or trivial, now cast in a new light by time or the perceptive choices of the creative collector.

❨ EMOTIONAL INVOLVEMENT

Collectors rush into burning buildings to save their treasures, have nervous breakdowns when they are stolen or broken, and spend sleepless nights dreading these and other calamities, because their emotions are involved.

Stories of collections put up for auction and then bought back by their owners, unable to bear parting with them, have punctuated the history of collecting for centuries. When collectors have actually killed to acquire certain pieces it has usually been attributed to greed, but when they have died to keep them, it could only be attributed to love. Petronius, drinking poison from the most prized drinking bowl in his collection and then dashing it to pieces to keep it from Nero, still stands as the most dramatic example, but not all instances of emotional involvement with collections are unhappy.

In writing of his collection of oriental ceramics, Sir Alan Barlow expresses a brighter aspect when he says, "The craftsman has impressed his personality on the lifeless clay. It almost ceases to be inanimate, it has breath and soul of its own, it is individual, unique; its very imperfections add to its allure." In the natural order of things, without calamities to cloud the horizon, collectors enjoy the pleasures of passion, are seldom betrayed, and build fine collections because they are in love with them.

The need to be needed is a factor in the emotional involvement of certain collectors. Some confer animistic qualities on their collections. A well-known clock collector likens the physical movement of a clock to the beating of the heart, and comments that a principal pleasure of collecting clocks is their "living" character.

Successful collectors see their entire collections as living organisms with which they are inextricably bound, and many have been known to shed wives and disinherit children, while continuing a deep emotional involvement with their treasures. Some imagine their collections to stand in the place of children, carrying on the collectors' names.

⟨ PURPOSEFUL

Obsessive is too strong a word, implying the irrational, so perhaps purposeful must serve to describe a principal characteristic of successful collectors, one that may also explain the high correlation of their achievements in other aspects of life. Whatever the source of the motivation, these individuals formulate an aim, plan and program in connection with it, and organize their energies and assets for the task of accomplishing it. This sense of purpose, of keeping an over-all goal in mind, gives direction to what might in collecting otherwise become merely agreeable dabbling.

Determined to know and collect ancient glass, Ray Winfield Smith, whose vocations included business and government service, became an amateur Egyptologist, leading authority on glass, and creator of a collection that took forty-five years in the formation and enriched great museums and private collections when dispersed in 1975. Chemistry, craftsmanship, design, dating, and geographical sources of his subject fell into the sweep of his purpose, and his ultimate object, to form a collection that showed the development, magnificent art and technique, and surpassing scope of glass from 1500 B.C. to A.D. 1200, was well accomplished.

His research, acquisition, and travel activities included arrangements for samples to be tested at atomic research facilities, for excavations, archaeological studies, and consultation with dealers and experts—serving as an outstanding example of purposeful collecting.

⟨ PERSISTENT

Except for the instant collector who occasionally acquires instant antiques, persistence and tenacity characterize the successful creator of collections.

Some, like James Lenox, amassing books, require a lifetime to fulfill a purpose that is never truly completed. Ralph Isham spent twenty-five years in pursuit of Boswell's papers, into castles, attics, and grain lofts, spending almost all his means as well, but persisting in his achievement of a remarkable collection.

Persistence takes many forms. Peggy Guggenheim's art collection illustrates one, whereby personal relationships with artists are pursued to shape a collection. Vintage auto collectors spend years searching for a particular type of flower vase to complete a car interior; a contemporary schoolboy will spend an entire vacation to find certain comic books to complete his collection.

Inevitable disappointments are met with resignation but never despair. Sometimes collectors have to wait for death to recycle in their favor. Persistence has been said to keep some alive to outlive the present possessor of a wanted treasure for a collection.

⟪ AND A LITTLE BIT OF LUCK

The truth is that those who are acquisitive, inquisitive, persistent, purposeful, quality-conscious, keen of judgment, skillful at trading, sensitive, visually alert, and emotionally involved in collecting are already lucky in having these traits.

However, when the blue glass liner actually fits the silver salt, the escutcheon matches, or the Bristol vase you find in the fleamarket is the only one missing from the garniture you own, the sense of good fortune, of being blessed by luck, adds a dimension of pleasure that enhances all others.

As in life, luck is not especially associated with virtue, but it makes those who are fortunate feel they have been selected because they are extraordinary. They say that is what keeps gamblers going, and perhaps this is so with collectors as well!

CHAPTER **12**

SOME CRIMES DO PAY

PENALTIES FOR counterfeiting precious metals and paper currency no longer include maiming, torture, or the death penalty, but are otherwise severe enough. However, those engaged in faking antiques, art, or collectibles would be drawn and quartered were they left to the tender mercies of collectors who had the misfortune to pay tribute to their skills. Dealers and others who trade in fakes would do little better, and consignment to that place in the Inferno arranged for them by Dante for counterfeiters would be considered far too good.

ꛙ COLLECTORS' VULNERABILITY

Actually, comparatively little punishment gets meted out to the perpetrators of the fraud and fakery that play such a large role on the collecting scene. Many victims never find out they have been fooled, many find out too late, and others are ashamed to publicly protest or take legal action. Most often the law is absent, unclear, or difficult or impossible to evoke. Only a small reflection of the full range of near or complete criminality in this field comes to light.

Supercollectors are the most vulnerable; hence they take the greatest precautions with expert advice. Like all collectors, they are stalked by the specter of fakery and fraud, and when they are taken in, the take is not insignificant. However, a large loss may play a smaller role in the financial situation of a wealthy collector than a lesser calamity to a modest one.

Nobody bothers to bite circulating coins these days, since they have become mere tokens of value, but some sort of testing for authenticity of old coins and practically everything else that is collected is an ongoing activity that promises to continue as long as there are collectors.

No area of collecting is impervious to deception by slightly shady to outright fraudulent methods. The most experienced, skillful, and wary collectors as well as experts admit to having been entrapped at some time. There is constant struggle for the integrity of every collection. The measures of deceit are as many as they are devious.

❲ HIDDEN REPAIRS

No halo surpasses the benediction of perfect condition, adding merit and value to every collection of anything. No item can merit the accolade of prime if it is battered, less than complete, scratched, or discolored. To simulate perfect condition brings an object into the circle of highest potential price, a paying proposition for restoration without admission, and a tempting one.

Therefore, authentic and original objects that have been damaged, a fact that may reduce value by as much as 90 per cent and completely destroy its appeal for most collectors, are cleverly repaired to conceal it.

Many other items, whose value is not so severely depressed, but which are still desirable despite some imperfections, are also treated to hidden repairs because the temptation to improve them and the price was too great to resist. In every case, it is to the advantage of the collector to know the true condition of each object acquired, in order to reckon its real value to the collection and its monetary value in terms of the collector's purse.

Porcelain and pottery, wood, paper, ivory, shell, enamel, and glass can be bonded with new glues that leave almost no trace to the naked eye. Minute study under a strong glass or X ray by "black light" reassures or ferrets out imperfections as well as hidden repairs.

Mended silver carries tales to the knowing who check for signs of soldering; yet if it is placed at a natural joining, it may be difficult to detect. Here change in color and patina are tipoff. Try breathing on a suspicious section—the area will stand in outline.

Authentic antique silver pieces with good hallmarks are "improved" by cutting away the ruined portions and forming the balance into lesser but still salable pieces.

All glass should be checked by daylight and artificial light as well. Here too, flaws and cracks are cut away or ground down.

Overpainting on canvas sometimes covers what is of even greater value, but more often it is deteriorated color or flaking paint that is thus masked.

When original old black-and-white prints are colored by contemporary hands, they are sold as "antique hand-colored prints," but not to the alert collector, who recognizes them as old but no longer authentic.

Little is as destructive in the sight of the expert frame collector as the flashy new gold-lacquered finish on a good old wood or gesso specimen. Repainting on old gesso frames is more difficult to remove than from wood.

Limited reweaving of fine carpets and other textiles is an acceptable repair. However, when carpets are painted, this is cheating. Experts watch out for carpets and rugs that have had worn borders removed, leaving the center, which is in good condition, as a remnant of much less value.

Furniture, wood boxes, wood sculpture, and what is called treen or woodenware are especially subject to hidden reconstruction to create more desirable items as well as to hide flaws.

Furniture repairs include replacing legs, splicing them, and changing shapes. Molding is replaced or added, sometimes pieced or decorated. Arms are added, turnings reshaped, restructured, or removed. Sides and fronts are replaced, aprons reshaped or recarved, carving added or reworked, and rails replaced. Table frames and hinges are replaced, as are butterfly supports and table pedestals. Tops of tables and chests are embellished by recarving, finials replaced and recarved on chairs and chests. Brasses may be replaced by old but not original units.

These above examples were from just thirty pieces of Early American furniture examined at Yale University in its study collection.

There are hundreds of other variations of furniture repair and restoration, each as subtle and invisible as a good artisan can make it.

"Marriages" occur in almost every type of antique. Parts from various original sources are mated to form bastards, which are not always even of the same period.

Serious collectors prefer, as do museums, a minimum of restoration, and that to be indicated. The collector who bought a fourteenth-century Chinese wine jar for $573,000 at a London auction saw that it had a visible crack and far preferred it to a hidden repair!

(RESTRIKES

Faint tones of authenticity serve as foundation for a sordid chicanery that cheats the buyer while damaging the reputation of the artist, as the original plates for lithographs, woodcuts, etchings, and other graphics are commercially reworked. When a legitimate limited edition has run its course, the plates are supposed to be destroyed or defaced, to prevent their future exploitation. Unfortunately, the temptation to resist destruction or to erase the marks of defacement sometimes overcomes integrity; the plates fall into greedy, questionable channels, and restruck prints appear on the market, claiming to be original.

If the plate itself was signed, the print may be offered, even advertised as a "signed, original," which it is not. To qualify as such, a limited-edition print must be hand pulled under the artist's supervision, and if the latter is satisfied that it has met a standard, signed in pencil and the number of the print and edition, sometimes the date, penciled in. There may be a series of editions on different paper, but they must be registered, differentiated, and signed by the artist to be original limited-edition prints. It has been reported that willing hands sign numbers and artists' names in the margins of restrikes. The collector will find authoritative lists of the prints of many artists' work, complete with the details of size of editions, to be helpful in sorting out the restrikes. Experts spot them by quality and sometimes by reworking of cross-marks intended for permanent defacement.

Coins are restruck and passed off as originals, often by foreign governments, taking advantage of the worldwide interest of hopefuls who want to hedge against inflation by buying rare coins and gold coins, without taking the trouble to become knowledgeable collectors.

One such restruck coin accounted for $45 million outflow in a single year from the United States to Hungary, according to the Department of Commerce. This gold coin, a restrike of a 1908 Imperial gold crown, would be worth about 10 per cent above its gold value, but was sold by dealers to collectors as a rare coin in mint condition, bringing very high prices. Since many investment buyers put such "numismatic portfolios" in a bank vault, it will be a sad day when they try to cash in on their "collections." Experts believe that this example is only one of many of the same kind.

While the United States Hobby Protection Act of 1974 made it a punishable offense to duplicate, import, or sell any coin or medal unless it is identified as a replica or restrike, experience indicates that the collector had best buy defensively with expertise, or from dealers whose guarantees are clear and responsibly backed. The government cannot stand over the shoulder of each purchaser.

In general, whenever an original mold, die, plate, or pattern of an original collectible is used for purposes of later issue or edition, the temptation is for some seller to claim it to be authentic. The buyer must learn to differentiate between primary and secondary value. In reading advertising, this means noting the fine print, and in handling an item, it means careful scrutiny for fine differences in quality and detail; sharpness in cut glass; color and weight in pottery and porcelain, hallmarks and patina in silver, texture of paper and fabric, and, whenever possible, in comparing the true original with the claimant object. Many books compare antiques, coins, books, stamps, and other collectibles, showing both the authentic originals and fakes and restrikes. However, while photographs and descriptions are helpful in alerting collectors, they are not substitutes for actual physical comparison.

Several thousand faked and altered coins form a collection amassed by the Organization of International Numismatists, and are used by that group in seminars for coin collectors and dealers. As such collections grow in every field, they will become the best of all defensive weapons.

(SURMOULAGE

Making new copies from existing casts, a type of sculpture reproduction formerly discussed in hushed and discrete fashion by art historians, museum curators, and supercollectors, has been brought into the open forum of public attention. It is now recognized that there are large numbers of unauthorized casts, whether made in the lifetime of the artist, or posthumously, which are falsely presented as originals, and considered by many experts to be a species of forgery.

Commercially merchandised museum reproductions, usually cast in plasticized stone, hardly need the identification they almost always bear. However, the quietly, even secretly made reproductions of important sculptures are another matter. It is said to be a common practice for the heirs or agents of sculptors to authorize posthumous casts, which may also be enlarged or made in smaller versions. Since the artists have never seen these, and have not had the opportunity to add the finishing touches, nor indeed to approve or reject, their standing as original works of art have been questioned. Examples such as a five-foot-tall papier-mâché pair of figures by Elie Nadelman, reproduced in stone with the height quadrupled, and of a cubist horse by Raymond Duchamp-Villon originally sixteen inches tall in plaster, later appearing in bronze in three different sizes, the largest five feet tall, indicate that not only the size, but also the medium is subject to posthumous change. Unauthorized reproduction in bronze, steel, and other metals of works originally executed in wax, wood, stone, or terra-cotta is becoming common.

The practice is defended by some who say that all of Degas' wax figures, cast in bronze after his death, are among the most important works in modern sculpture. However, it would seem that the storm of controversy broke after it was discovered that some collectors and dealers were acquiring sculptures such as Matisse and Giacometti originals, having them cast in duplicate, and selling these as originals. To some experts, it is the question of surreptitious casting that is at the heart of the collector's dilemma in this matter. Whether or not it is authorized and by whom, may settle the problem of the so-called authentic fake. In any case, the collector who acquires a piece of sculpture should have the privilege of knowing how the artist originally conceived it, how many so conceived were issued by him or her as an original version and so documented.

(WRONG ATTRIBUTIONS

In many cases, research uncovers information that leads to re-attribution, certainly a legitimate and necessary pursuit, one the collector approves as worthy and often joins. The silver bowl has not changed, but if it turns out that the maker was not the great Myer Myers, but one of the many silversmiths of the same or slightly later period who were lesser MM's, the market says "sorry," and the bowl immediately becomes worth about half on that market.

Tiffany, Lalique, Galle, Steuben, Waterford, Baccarat, Hawkes, Dorflinger, Sandwich, and even Northwood can all be wrongly attributed to the advantage of the seller. Marks alone can be more easily added than quality, and clever collectors buy on the basis of the virtues of the piece rather than the fame of the maker, paying for attribution only when it is unquestioned.

The Louvre once organized a major exhibition under the title "Copies, Replicas, and Pastiches" of over a hundred paintings, to demonstrate that there are many ways in which a work may be authentic, although not the original, unique product of a single artist. The exhibition also included a number of deliberate forgeries, but it was for the more subtle and complicated aspects that it particularly contributed to the understanding of collectors' problems in other areas as well as painting.

Frequently artists copied their own paintings several times in slightly varying versions. They also copied other artists' work, sometimes in their own interpretations, sometimes exactly. Ingres collaborated with pupils; one example shown was executed by him with two of his pupils, another was painted entirely by a pupil.

Both paintings bear Ingres' signature. Rubens was said to have charged his clients according to how much of a painting he himself, rather than his assistants, executed, but he signed the whole, no matter what the proportion.

⟨ ALTERED DATES

Occasionally these are merely "circas" that are optimistically slanted to a more desirable era, and may be a matter of opinion, so given. However, when a date is *changed*, then even an original may not be the real thing it purports to be. Often items are "improved," as when hallmarks on English silver are altered to make a piece seem older and more desirable. Coins can be tampered with, 3's changed to 8's and 5's to 6's, always to simulate greater rarity and value. This is fraud, and collectors who do not recognize the perils of the numbers game are the more easily victimized.

⟨ PHONY PAPERS

It is still a lively tradition for complaisant dealers to furnish as many differently priced bills as the buyer-collector requires. One may be for tax or customs purposes, one for insurance or appraisal purposes, one to show the complaining spouse, and perhaps even a correct figure for private records. Bills are definitely documentation, but hardly incontrovertible.

Costly works and objects of art, antiquities, and antiques have long been subject to demand on the part of the buyer for certification by experts. In the past, highly respected authorities were paid well for these documents, and still are for such authentication. The papers themselves add greatly to the value of the object in question, and have thus become objects of value as well, tempting some to buy and others to sell them. It is not unusual for shady dealers and their experts to create imaginary collections from which works of unknown provenance are supposed to come.

When several London dealers bought Greek vases on the basis of forged papers, supposedly from the British Museum, authorities of that institution expressed consternation on two grounds. The failure of the buyers to check the documents, which they could so easily do in London, indicated that their circulation abroad would be even easier to accomplish successfully. The second presumption was that the dealers, on selling the vases to collectors, would "guarantee" in writing that they were authentic, based on supposed assurance from museum experts, thus reflecting discredit on the institution.

A famous archaeologist publicly announced his pleasure in seeing the dealers cheated. He thought that their willingness to buy on such slim documentation without checking, encouraged thefts from archaeological sites. He hoped that this example might discourage them.

In attempting to stop the flood of Latin American national archaeological treasures from being stolen for export and often purchased by museums as well as private collectors, the United States requires an export license from the country of origin. However, the temptation to forge such certificates has brought up another problem: What expertise does a museum official or collector have to check whether the signature of Juan Gomez is authentic?

⟦ "MISTAKEN" APPRAISALS

In seeking an appraiser for a collection, for items under consideration for insurance, estate decisions, acquisition, or sale, the collector is often recommended to a dealer in the field. Aside from the temptation to undervalue on the chance that the material may be offered for purchase, many dealers are simply not equipped with the expertise to cover a wide range of antiques, art, or collectibles. It is essential that the appraiser have experience in the field in question.

An antiques silver specialist will often buy and sell old jewelry without knowing how to identify or value rare pieces of the latter, yet would gladly accommodate a client in appraising for insurance purposes. Even in dealing with leading auction firms, it is necessary to be sure in which area the employee or member of the firm is expert. Should a member of a particular department be on vacation, your appraisal would be done by someone else whose "educated guess" might be very much off the mark. Most smaller auction firms have general appraisers, well experienced, but rarely expert in any single field.

⟨ FAKES AND FORGERIES

The need for checking controversial items with the newest scientific techniques was illustrated when Yale University announced that its treasured "Vinland Map," which showed North America as discovered by Leif Ericson centuries before Columbus, to be a forgery. Although some had questioned the map for which an anonymous donor had paid almost a million dollars, prior methods of analysis would have required such large samples of the parchment and ink that the map would have been destroyed. It was only when new methods required ink specks so small they could not be seen by the naked eye, that the tests that proved it a forgery could be made. They established the presence of materials in the ink that could not have been produced before the 1920s.

Nor are forgeries confined to million-dollar maps and similar costly treasures. Twentieth-century Japanese ceramics, known to collectors as "O.J." for their marking indicating Occupied Japan, are not immune either. This bric-a-brac, produced from 1945 to 1951, much of it made for variety chain stores and gift shops, usually hand-painted in bright and garish colors, has been ardently collected. A large following, a small literature, and the omnipresent price guides have appeared in its trail. The distress of the collectors of this specialty, when they found that the mark was appearing on items from Taiwan, Korea, Hong Kong, and postoccupation Japan, was no less severe because the individual sums involved were comparatively modest.

In turn, pattern glass, Tiffany and other Art Glass, scrimshaw and African tribal art have been honored by attempts to fake them. When Leica camera collectors, in search of specific models to complete collections, began to pay enough to make it interesting, models worth $225 were converted to units for which ten times that much was gladly paid. Since some collections of the complete Leica series were worth as much as $250,000, and collectors were paying as much as $15,000 for rare models, there was an unsuccessful attempt to keep the news of the swindles hushed. Thus, in certain cases, the mere act of producing counterfeits may serve as a sort of blackmail, with victims preferring to keep silent to protect their total investment in collections.

(FANTASIES

Not all fakes are nearly or exactly like the items that they attempt to be taken for. Some clever forgers prefer to offer truly "original" objects that are in-the-manner-of rather than duplicates. Paperweights, milk glass, *Frakturs*, pottery in almost every field, trivets, political buttons, antique tools, American Indian jewelry and rugs, and manuscripts, to say nothing of paintings by famous artists, are among the innumerable fantasies that approximate rather than copy. In some way, experts say these are harder to spot, because if the feeling is right and the material has been carefully prepared to indicate the right age, it takes even more study to reconcile or reject offbeat examples, which are likely to occur in every field.

(FAKING SIGNS OF AGE

Not only objects, but their collectors are distressed by fakers, the latter when the signs of age are successfully faked on the former. Wood can be dried, even fried; copper and brass dipped, dripped, and banged; fabrics dyed and bleached; glass buried or discolored by chemicals; carpets kept in animal stalls, and ivory dipped in licorice and nicotine. The ingenuity and cunning of tricksters in faking signs of age has endless variations, developed through centuries of experience. It is the counterpart to hidden repairs and restoration.

When the work is done skillfully, it may present problems, but comparison with authentic examples that show signs of wear and age will usually point up differences. Here again, specialization in forming a collection gives the collector access to books and articles that have explored the techniques of fakers, as well as to experts and conservators for advice.

(REPRODUCTIONS

To complete this roster of guile, reproductions come in not one, but several categories. The most obvious are mass-produced commercial reproductions. Although they may make no claim to being vintage objects or antiques at the source, some are clearly marked to indicate their origins; others are not. Even in this instance, firms with long traditions may rightfully continue to use their prestigious names; it is up to the buyer to know how to differentiate marks and examples of old and new Wedgwood, Lenox, Hitchcock, Tiffany, and many similar great makers. Some of these also make their own authorized reproductions, properly marked, but sometimes marks are changed or deleted by others.

Manufacturers and importers, ever alert to sales possibilities, note that an item has become a popular collectible, undertake to reproduce it, possibly selling it at a fair commercial price, but leaving it for the dealer to erase or otherwise delete telltale marks. More or less innocently made as a reproduction, an object can be more or less easily sold as an original.

Watching commercial retail outlets, trade paper advertisements to dealers, and noting when many dealers offer the same "antique" are protective devices that hone detecting skills.

"Aged reproductions," often in themselves collectible to the knowledgeable who acquire them at a price in line with their true value, are hazards to the unwary. Furniture, paintings, silver, glass, ceramics, coins, jewelry, and copper and brass items were often copied in the far-distant past for various reasons. In the Renaissance they wanted to emulate the antique because they admired it; then and later, it became considered a mark of homage to copy an antique. Beautiful objects and art, especially paintings, were ordered copied by their owners until the eighteenth century, to present as gifts. In Victorian times, period fine French furniture was copied because there wasn't enough of the original to go around. Occasionally a duplicate was required to make a pair or several pieces ordered to complete a dozen in silver.

To this day, fine custom reproductions slip into the antiques market as a wealthy individual needing money secretly sells the

original of a fine piece of furniture and uses some of the price to
have it replaced by an exact copy, often made in the workrooms
of the dealer who buys it. Not even the heirs know, and if it
should be sold privately or even at auction, it may well pass as an
original. Dealers say it takes about fifty years to absorb such reproductions, which often become enshrined in other collections and
even museums.

⟨ STOLEN TREASURES

The increasing amount of space allotted by collectors' publications to the ads and queries about objects stolen from collectors
and dealers reflects the growing hazards of ownership, but they indicate another danger as well. Buying stolen collectibles can be
both unpleasant and unprofitable, as many innocent buyers who
have had to give up the prize without getting their money back
can attest.

Since title to stolen goods is never secure, the buyer who does
not use every prudent method for assurance of previous ownership
and the right of the seller to make the sale is not only creating a
potential problem in regard to that purchase, but is also encouraging the movement of stolen goods that may some day be his or
her own!

The freedom with which stolen items are offered for sale was indicated when the FBI advertisement listing items in a $100,000
collection theft coincided with auction advertisements offering the
same items of silver, antique jewelry, and art objects. Had the
thieves been less ambitious in their choice of sales outlet, they
might indeed have had fewer problems and the purchasers more.

⟨ SELF-SWINDLED

In addition to the tricks, hoaxes, frauds, and misrepresentations
that are practiced on collectors, the collectors are susceptible to
another sort of misfortune. This is self-inflicted, born of hope,
nurtured by anxiety, and tainted by covetousness. The collector so
urgently wishes the object to be what is wanted and wants it so

immoderately as to believe without sufficient evidence of authenticity, true condition or attribution, or even actual ownership. Often it is not necessary for a trap or plot to be laid, but generally there are classic techniques to encourage self-entrapment. Often the collector is in a hurry to buy before the dealer or owner really finds out its "true" value, an easy trick to stage, and one that unscrupulous dealers have been working for centuries.

CHAPTER **13**

RESEARCH WITHOUT TEARS

RESEARCH IS A heavy word from which many collectors recoil. Yet as purchasers of ten-speed bicycles, fur coats, or waterproof watches, they automatically make surveys about these objects that would translate into terms of research were they about antiques, art, or other collectibles.

In general, both the degree of curiosity and the energy to pursue it are elements that vary in each collector's personality. Some are satisfied with superficial information about the subject of the collection and the objects within it, while others steep themselves in constant study and investigation. Most fit into neither extreme, having some information and intending to acquire more, but rarely taking the initiative, unaware of the simple measures and methods by which they could enrich and develop their collections.

⟨ VERBAL SOURCES

Ask the seller or the source to tell you what is known about the object, lacing reliance on the reply with a healthy dose of skepticism.

Don't ask "Is it old?"; ask "How old is it?" The first question implies you know nothing, the second that you are checking yet not challenging.

Word-of-mouth inquiry can be valuable, but it is not always reliable. Consider the disinterestedness of your informant.

Base your confidence on common sense. You aren't too likely to get much insight on the techniques of making cloisonné when you buy a cloisonné vase at a tag sale. However, you might be told it was bought on a trip to the Orient "the year we were married," indicating something about its age.

Ask if there are letters, photos, or bills from that trip. They may just have them. Mark any papers relating to acquisition and your notes on verbal information with dates.

If you buy in a shop, get a description of the item on the letterhead with as much information as the dealer will give you as to origins, history, and authenticity.

Since no one knows everything about everything, the advantage is with the specialist collector. Anyone can learn a lot about something.

The individual bits of information you acquire will accrue to form a solid base on which to add more. That's how experts are formed.

Examine and handle items in your field whenever you can. Use a magnifying glass; if necessary, acquire a jeweler's loup.

Auctions and exhibitions are good ground for field work. Ask dealers for permission to examine items in their stocks.

Even if you can't afford to be an important customer, visit, talk with, and learn from the top dealers in a field. You can't continue without making an occasional small purchase, but if you include the value of an ongoing education, it will be a bargain.

(SETTING IT DOWN

Getting a written or signed description will not preclude fantasy, but it will inhibit it.

Start with a simple alphabetical folder for all information with reference to the collection. You may want to expand later, but these and a looseleaf notebook will do for a while.

State the source as you make notes of the information required. Some may be wrong; you'll know who to blame.

Define what you want to know about an item. You may flounder and get discouraged without a clear purpose.

Tracing a manufacturer, a patent number, the dates spanning an artist's or artisan's lifetime, the kind of threads used in certain textiles, and the name of a cut-glass design will be the average problems.

Carry a list of the specific questions for which you seek answers, together with a snapshot or sketch.

What is it called?
When was it made?
Who was the maker or manufacturer?
What do the marks signify?
How was it used?
Does the design or style have a name?
By what process was it made?
Is it an original?
Is it rare or common?
Is it complete or part of a set?
Does it have historical significance?
Is it an early example or a prototype?
Who owned it originally? Later?
Are there similar items in existing collections? Where?

⟨ COLLECTING KNOWLEDGE

Dealers who are best informed have the best-stocked bookshelves. Although librarians will be helpful in recommending books, dealers, who are usually willing to let you copy the titles, authors, and publishers of their much-used references, have the advantage of grass-roots experience.

Many important reference books on antiques, art, and other subjects of interest to collectors may be out of print. Check with specialist booksellers who hunt them down for you.

Building a specialized library is truly the best investment a collector can make as an aid to forming a collection. In addition to its principal purpose, it is a good investment; as some of the books go out of print, they themselves become collectors' rarities.

In addition to the outstanding books on a subject, articles, brochures, pamphlets, and catalogs of all sorts constitute valuable reference material for which collectors should be alert.

Dealer-experts and specialists will guide, but collectors must also study. You can learn by asking, but you can only pick others' brains to a point.

If the collector simply accepts, and does not probe the reasons for a dealer's judgment, does not compare and evaluate independently, an opportunity for growth is lost.

The role of one dealer as an all-knowing guru has limitations. Get perspective from various sources.

A growing number of young dealers are college-trained in research. One, whose graduate projects crossed political with art history, specializes in American and English historical antiques of the eighteenth and nineteenth centuries.

Prices such as $300 for a photograph of Lincoln paired with a mourning ribbon worn at his funeral; an English pitcher with an abolition motif at $700; and a suffragette poster for $225, indicate that historical research pays.

❪ FIRST THE BOOK

The old slogan "Buy the book before the coin" can be usefully transposed into every field of collecting, but there are many reference books in public libraries, including guides and directories to aid the collector who prefers their free facilities.

Dealers and their specialties
Mastai's Classified Directory, U.S. and Canada

Experts, private collectors, private collections, museums
International Directory of Arts

Collections in American museums
Official Directory of American Association of Museums

Lists of reference collections in U.S. libraries
Subject Collections

Specialized sources can be located and evaluated through these guides

The American Reference Books Annual   B. S. Wynar

Guide to Reference Books   Constance M. Winchell

Home Reference Books in Print   S. P. Walsh

Reference Books: A Brief Guide for Students and Other Users of the Library   Barton and Bell

Periodical articles on collecting

Ayer's Directory

Ulrich's International Periodicals Directory

Review columns of special-interest magazines will recommend and evaluate reference and topical books of interest to collectors in their own fields.

❬ VARIETY OF SOURCE MATERIALS

Collectors wanting to keep up to date on newest scientific discoveries and experts' opinions will have to read collectors' periodicals, where they usually appear first.

When experts claimed new attributions and dates for Japanese antique porcelains, the articles appeared in specialist periodicals.

Museums exchange their own publications with other institutions. In many cases these are available for the public to read in museum reference libraries.

Old diaries, wills, account books, newspapers, and town directories, often on file in historical society libraries, are especially useful for tracing Americana of the eighteenth through the early twentieth centuries.

Sales catalogs, advertising material, tags, labels, and old-timers' recollections offer research opportunities. Old Sears, Roebuck catalogs are much in demand.

Even if the material is not permitted to circulate from a library, ask for permission to make a single duplicate copy of crucial pages for your files.

When Frances Phipps restored the kitchen of her 1742 Connecticut house, she used old household inventories, settlers' journals, travelers' diaries, letters, books, and newspaper accounts of the period to guide her.

❡ PRIVATE AND PUBLIC EXPERTS

Sir Alan Barlow said that his expertise on Chinese pottery depended on consultation with archaeologists, students of costume, calligraphy, religion, and philosophy. He also consulted experts in textiles and bronzes as well as chemists and physicists.

Professionals will test and examine the canvas and paint, brush strokes, markings, patina, subject, stretcher, and then top that with X-ray technology. Collectors who want this sort of research must pay for it.

The great art expert Morelli never accepted a signature until he had checked the work. How an artist painted thumbs was sometimes his test of attribution.

Lest the beginning, or even advanced collector become discouraged when origins prove difficult to trace, the following from the University of London Courtauld Institute Galleries shows that even disagreeing experts admit to being baffled.

General Catalogue of the Courtauld Institute Galleries, University of London.   pg. 17.

Description of painting #34 from the Gambier-Parry Collection

The Story of St. Quiricus and St. Julitta (3 separate panels)

Tempera on panel

"The three panels were bought with an attribution to Masaccio but in selling them Spence added a note that they were 'perhaps by Masolino da Panicale.' They were exhibited at the Royal Academy in 1930 under the label of the Florentine School, early fifteenth century. On this occasion Roger Fry, somewhat surprisingly, ascribed them to the young Pesollino—an attribution accepted by Constable—and records the suggestion of an unnamed colleague that they might be by Brunelleschi. Berenson attributed them to an artist 'Between Masaccio Ucello and Castagno,' Kaftal to one between Masaccio and Masolino. More recently Longhi created a 'Master of St. Quiricus and St. Julitta' named after the Gambier-Parry panels, to whom he also attributed a Madonna and Saints in the Saglietti collection, Bologna, and whom he defines as a follower of Masaccio working about the 1430s.

"It has also been suggested that the painting, although evidently Tuscan, is not necessarily Florentine, and it has been pointed out that one of the very few churches dedicated to St. Quiricus is . . . in Siena. . . ."

Taking heart from the above, the private collector whose insecure attributions cannot be positively proven, should persevere in tracing trivets, mesh purses, cameras, or carpets. Intelligent opinions are better than none.

Private collectors, as part of the general public, can benefit from the expertise of scholars who are paid by our government.

The Library of Congress employs some of the best-trained, most scholarly authorities in many areas. Various posts are filled by experts who have spent an entire lifetime working in a specialty.

The collector who uses the Division of Prints and Photographs finds a file catalog devised by an expert who has handled each of the more than one hundred thousand graphics individually.

Each print in the Library of Congress Catalog is arranged according to chronology and geography, and carries notes on conditions, states, and collectors' marks.

Libraries, museums, and universities throughout the world offer the collector in search of information the benefits of invaluable scholarship, often for the mere effort of requesting them.

❲ RANGE OF RESEARCH

In addition to the standard art collections, colleges and universities as well as private foundations are forming instructive collections of what many call trivia and ephemera or vintage nostalgia.

Originally it was believed that American folk design and decoration was an independent expression of rural life. It now appears from research that urban inspiration in the form of prints, woodcuts, engravings, and even technical manuals were prototype sources.

Great masses of material were inventoried and classified and the originals from which the folk artists drew inspiration were identified.

As more material is checked out and perhaps other theories develop, they too may be challenged. However, the collector who keeps up with current research can shape a better and more valuable collection

A professor at Harvard was quoted, "It's like a clinic here at the Fogg Art Museum . . . we see them all and we're courteous . . . there must be constant practice in this work."

When experts will only tell you that your possession is "very interesting," you are being politely signaled that they believe it to be of very little consequence.

There was a grand old style, even in methods of research. When John Jones, the great Victorian collector of Sevres, questioned the unusual blue tint of a vase he had bought, he immediately sent it by hand from London to the factory in France. There the original century-old mold and documents were checked and his waiting messenger given written assurances that the piece was genuine!

❦ COUNT ON THE COMPUTER

A century later, computers are beginning to bring electronic techniques into the field of collecting research. However, the individual collector will continue to set the standards and creative directions for each collection, and has to formulate the right questions before the information in the machine can be useful in forming collections.

An obstacle to those engaged in accumulating data about collections is the reticence of some owners who do not want records of their ownership in such channels for fear of Internal Revenue Service tax problems, or assets available to creditors, relatives, or burglars. In deference to their problems, the desire to remain an anonymous owner is respected by responsible compilers.

Data banks, stored in computers, herald a future when the collector need only pose a question, punch some keys, and retrieve the desired information. The Computer Museum Network, a nonprofit organization with headquarters at the New York State University Center in Stony Brook, Long Island, New York, has developed a system to house information about works of art, artifacts, and documentary material. Twenty museum affiliates contributed to the establishment of the computer system, including the Museum of Modern Art, Metropolitan Museum of Art, and the National Gallery of Art in Washington.

This project is based on direct information linkage between the member institutions and involved setting up computer terminals at each institution connected to a central information bank. The researcher sits in front of a small TV-like screen, punches keys, and watches the display of the retrieved information. This system has been programmed to provide a physical description of a piece, data on the artist or artisan, the owner, previous owner, location of a work, and in some cases, the price for which it was acquired.

Another interesting use of electronic information to aid the collector is a project known as the Bicentennial Inventory, funded by the U. S. Government for the National Collection of Fine Arts, a part of the Smithsonian Institution. The goal is to record every American oil, watercolor, fresco, pastel, or painting in any medium whatsoever, made before 1914.

Started in 1970, the project is eventually expected to record at least a million works of art. This catalog, for that is what it is, makes no value judgment; it is strictly historical. The title, name of artist, date created, medium, material, dimensions, present ownership if stated, location, and if possible a photograph of the work, form the body of information sought and recorded and housed in the building of the Archives of American Art in Washington, D.C. 20560.

Lost masterpieces are turning up. An Indiana high school produced a Russell buffalo chase, a Remington Indian battle, some Hudson River School paintings, and a portrait of George Washington attributed to Gilbert Stuart. When dozens of photographs of the work of a nineteenth-century artist hitherto unknown outside of Michigan were sent in response to the questionnaire, the National Collection staff was impressed and arranged a show of Horace Shaw's work for other collectors' information.

Many new areas will open to collectors as data on shapes, symbols, subjects, and materials continue to be fed into computers and the facts organized to tell their relationships and origins. It will be some time before all fields are covered, but the individual collector can discover if computer data banks have been developed in the category of a particular interest by inquiring from those already in existence or from the prime manufacturers and leasers of computer equipment.

Government data banks will eventually furnish printouts of requested information by mail, and cross-indexing under many headings will be a valuable research tool.

CHAPTER 14

ORGANIZING YOUR COLLECTION

❨ PUT IT ON THE RECORD
❨ PUT IT ON THE REGISTER
❨ MAKING A DOSSIER   ❨ PHOTOGRAPH IT
❨ MARK IT   ❨ SECURE IT
❨ IN CASE OF THEFT   ❨ MOVING AND PACKING
❨ INSURANCE PROTECTION

THOSE MOMENTS when the auctioneer says "Gone" to your bid, when the dealer hands you the precious package, or when the object is gently cradled in the trunk of your car may be exciting and triumphant, but the private ceremony at home, when the object is scrutinized, admired, and absorbed, has extra and deeper dimensions. Having sought, found, chosen, carefully examined, valued, bargained for, and acquired their treasures, collectors turn from the role of courting lover to possessive spouse. It is as though one phase of a relationship were closed and another assumed, offering pleasure, but not without responsibility.

Whether the object is a century-old photograph, pewter flagon, Indian feather basket, pressed glass bottle, oriental ivory carving, or Belter settee, care, conservation, storage, and display are part of the ongoing protective process that ownership of a collection or individual collectibles entails. Supercollectors and institutions have their official curators; the rest of us must be self-employed caretakers.

❡ PUT IT ON THE RECORD

The care, nurture, and "feeding" of collections will necessarily vary with materials and the objects themselves, but there are certain procedures, most of them established within this century, that public and private collections follow to safeguard and enhance their values. While some of the procedures may seem to require greater resources than are generally available, they can all be approximated, and with some effort and ingenuity, adjusted to individual capacity as well as requirements.

Having enjoyed the unisex delights of transporting a possession over the threshold, the savvy collector begins the joys of domesticity by making a record for files that are already in, or about to commence existence. Whatever the destiny of a collection, whether it endures or is dissipated and recycled, its very existence, however transitory, contributes to the general fund of human knowledge and experience. This refers not only to the obviously important collections, seen by many people and handsomely enshrined in fine catalogs, or at the least, recorded as auction lot numbers when sold, but also to the countless individual collections that might never be published, but that could be described with a degree of permanence, through notebooks, albums, and photographs.

Museums and supercollections register the entry of each object the day of arrival, with a necessary minimum of information, and soon after catalog or describe it completely. The average collector might do well to set up a procedure of immediately entering everything then known about the item, and later adding what is learned by further examination, study, and comparison. Actually, the importance of making an entry on the date of arrival is stressed for the amateur collector, partly because if it is not done then, it will probably be postponed and often forgotten. In addition, details are often blurred and names confused after an interval. While it might not turn out to be critical, the last owner's recollection that an overlay decanter was brought to Cincinnati from Bohemia in 1854 by a relative who fled after taking part in the uprisings of 1848, would be a circumstance worth noting. The name might be forgotten were it not immediately recorded, and should you later read about an American Civil War officer by that name and similar antecedents, your record would have the distinction of contributing to historical research.

Not everyone will rival the collector of 15,000 pitchers, or of 845 travelers' sewing kits, but when any collection passes a few score mark, it needs to be kept under control in some fashion.

⟨ PUT IT ON THE REGISTER

Looseleaf pages in a notebook, card files, or individual folders will serve the same purpose. They organize what is known about each object listed and record its location, after receiving an accession number, usually in order of acquisition.

A portfolio of four prints or a five-piece tea set would each be given a single accession number, plus an addition decimal for each unit. Thus if the accession number were 84, the first print would be 84.1 and the second 84.2 until all were recorded.

In addition to each item in the tea set having its proper decimal, the removable parts are given letters. The teapot would be 95.1 (a) if it had a removable lid.

❲ MAKING A DOSSIER

A standard registration form used by museums in the interim before the item is cataloged with more substantial information carries the following:

Identification number
Source
Date of entry
Description
Condition
Price or estimated value
Location on premises
Purpose (study, loan, exhibit)
Disposition

No contemporary museum registrar is likely to follow the tragic example of Abraham Vanderdort, keeper of the cabinet for King Charles I. Vanderdort misplaced a miniature and hanged himself when he couldn't find it. It was discovered safely put away shortly thereafter. "Location on premises" carefully noted is considered the best safeguard against aggravation, at the least.

A registration form used by an art museum devoted entirely to painting, graphics, and sculpture indicates the importance of descriptive dimensional identification in addition to details such as location of signature.

Museum number
Date and place received
Date returned and accepted

Source
Credit line
Artist
Title
Place and date

Medium
Surface

Support: Dimensions
Mount: "
Mat: "
Frame: "
Base: "
Case: "

Location of signature
Marks

Price
Insurance valuation
Photo negative
History

Date insured
Voucher

A typical catalog form for a large private collection or museum
is somewhat more complex:

Accession number
Descriptive heading (chair, tapestry, painting)
Artist
Title of work
Heraldry
Inscription
Signature
Date of signature
Maker's mark
Material and measurements
Name of donor or vendor
Price if purchase
Valuation if gift
Ex collection
Provenance
Period and style
Designer name and dates

Place made
Place found
Age
Period and style
Photo

Because of the variety of material, the registration form or dossier for each item that might possibly come into a general museum, has a broader base than one as specialized as the picture and sculpture example, or a collection of toys, canes, or any other more limited category.

Collectors of antiques, works of art, curios, and other collectibles will develop their own dossier forms, with emphasis on individual specifications and pertinent information.

Some collectors of costly objects have been known to keep their home records in code form so thieves would not have the advantage of a guided plan for burglary should they break in and find them.

Duplicate records and photographs stored outside the structure in which the collection is kept form a safeguard in case of fire and other catastrophes as well.

Purchase records are considered so essential to the value of a collection that the originals are kept with other valuable records.

❲ PHOTOGRAPH IT

Photographs are evidence, should an item be damaged, proof if it should be stolen, identification by which it can be traced, assurance for insurance purposes, a historical record, and on occasion of disposal, can serve to help in the sale.

A recognizable photograph serves to refresh the memory; it is also useful for research and inquiry.

Museums and supercollections as well as some dealers have photographers on staff, but even if only a simple camera is available, so does every collector on his or her own person.

Colored slides that can be enlarged into color prints are recommended as economical and versatile.

Experts say that photographer-collectors will find that cable cord that screws into the shutter button and a tripod with crank-operated center post will help overcome blurring.

Good, clear prints are well lit, and a light meter, photofloods, or flash units are recommended equipment.

Dark objects should be photographed on light ground and light objects on dark ground. One expert suggests that background fabric be in keeping with items. Silver on velvet, treen on burlap, and inkwells on blotters are appropriate.

Close-up lenses are required for collections of miniatures and small items such as jewelry, coins, and stamps.

A wide space between object and background, and a frosted cover over the flash, even filling vessels with water will help make photos of glass objects sharper.

Professional museum photographers customarily use smaller photos from 8x10 glossies and mount them on cards.

Museums mark negatives with accession numbers; also, sometimes the negative number of the record photograph appears on the card.

Some collectors consider the photographs the unique record of the collection and note the cost and purchase date on the back of each photo, making duplicate copies for backup.

Where measurements are required, it is customary to consistently record dimensions in the same order. The preferred notation is height, length, width, and depth in sequence.

The widest points are customarily used; should there be variation in the form, it is noted. If a teapot with its cover are given as the total height, this is explained.

⟨ MARK IT

Ideally, each object would be so unique that if properly described and photographed, and its ownership recorded, this would prove sufficient to identify it if lost or stolen. However, few collections consist of remarkable rarities.

If an item is lost or stolen, the ability to point to a mark identifying it as the property of the claimant can be very helpful. Marked items are also harder for thieves to sell.

A certain ambivalence about permanently marking objects in a collection arises because the purists consider that any difference from the original state reduces the desirability of an item.

In recording the description of an object, such factors as monograms, hallmarks, ceramic marks, signatures, and patent or registry numbers are essential.

Repairs, imperfections, and areas of wear are important identifying characteristics. Museums even count and position flyspecks (unfortunately, these can be permanent) on a canvas and the number of dowels in each drawer of a chest.

Many coins and stamps are dependent on absolutely unblemished condition for their great value. For these, tamperproof holders that can be indelibly marked are considered a partial solution.

Collectors are reticent about etching identifying marks with electric engravers recommended by the police, but for many items where it can be done unobtrusively, and without detraction from value, they are doing so.

Tags and labels are too easily detached; glue and plastic tape may even cause some objects to deteriorate. New methods for marking are required.

Professional techniques of marking without effecting damage to an object vary in permanence, but if discreetly applied, may not be observed. These marks are usually numbers and letters that collate with records and files.

Artists' oil colors are used to mark   glass
                                        metal
                                        ceramics
                                        wood

The oil paint, generally used in vermilion or cadmium red, is slightly thinned with turpentine. These colors are used to make the numbers stand out. The private collector may prefer an opposite effect, making them unobtrusive.

To make the marks adhere better to smooth surfaces, lacquer thinner instead of turpentine is used, with a few drops of clear lacquer added.

Should the surface be of porous (usually old) wood, a thin layer of shellac will avoid absorption.

After the figures have dried, they are often protected with a coat of shellac.

Permanent markings can be made with India ink, used over water base paint that has dried. Later, a coat of shellac will seal.

Linen tape is sewed on for textiles, although fabrics and rugs may carry secret stitch marks.

Paper objects can be lightly marked in medium lead pencil; never "indelible" anything!

Museums stamp prints on the reverse side, using great care to avoid the mark showing through the paper. They use small rubber stamps with their monograms or names with a dark brown printer's ink.

Small objects should be numbered near the base. Heavy objects should never be marked on the bottom. Mark scroll paintings on the knob of the scroll.

Paintings are conventionally numbered on the reverse of the lower corner of the stretcher and frame. In some places it is customary to also mark on the reverse upper left corner as well, so one can be checked when the picture is hanging, the other when stacked.

⟨ SECURE IT

There was a time when collectors of cut glass, dolls, quilts, or weathervanes might feel more secure from burglary than those whose collections consisted of gold coins, jewels, or masterpiece paintings. This is no longer the case, as collectors', dealers', and even museums' losses escalate in every category.

Elaborate security systems are costly and thus not available to all collectors, yet the modest collector also feels threatened and anxious.

Supercollectors struggle between ego and prudence, very often making purchases, loans, and even gifts "anonymously."

Even in the lower echelons, many collectors feel that the best evasive action is privacy that takes on the aspects of secrecy. Neighbors, acquaintances, tradespeople, even younger members of the family are screened from awareness that a collection exists.

In general, all collectors are advised to secure their homes with the minimum precautions taken by any prudent householder.

Solid doors, window closures, automatic lighting, and avoidance
of outward indications of absence are basic.

Some types of collections or parts of them can be kept in bank
vaults and storage warehouses for safety when home security
measures are inadequate.

Hiding collections in the house requires collector's ingenuity
and poses interesting and sometimes amusing challenges. Burglars
are said to be contemptuous of the average householder's originality, but collectors who don't even tell one another try harder
and do better.

Inquiries originating from unknown sources should be turned
away with information that the collection has been sold, donated,
or is in storage.

In addition to engineering as much safety into the premises as
possible, collectors are advised that strangers asking to see the
collection should be doublechecked as to their bona fides and, if
possible, "accidentally" photographed.

Some collectors, unhappy at developing into suspicious and even
paranoid personalities, resist by simply insuring their collections
and acting with normal prudence.

A leading gun collector who had become obsessed with the dangers of burglary lived with complex security systems, kept his address a secret, and feared to leave home. Becoming a virtual rec-
luse and finding all this too much, he sold his whole collection!

([IN CASE OF THEFT

Authorities often complain that collectors are sometimes slow to
report theft or burglary. It is believed that many do not report at
all.

Delay favors the criminal. A stolen antique chair was resold three times in two states in a single day.

Reluctance to inform authorities of loss can be caused by fear of embarrassment when a spouse learns of the value of a collection hitherto deemed minimal.

Advertising the loss in collectors' periodicals will be most effective if accompanied by photos and detailed descriptions.

(MOVING AND PACKING

A primary rule of protection is that transportation of treasures is best avoided; the less moving and churning the better.

Yet trade and exchange, the movement of collections in whole or part, en route to new ownership change of location for other reasons, form an inescapable part of collecting activity. Though the question whether any trip is necessary is a good one, the answer cannot always be in the negative.

Museums, often involved in lending and borrowing for exhibition, are cutting back on such projects due to excessive cost and the fear of damage, but together with insurance companies and carriers as well as expert packers, continue to work on advancing safety techniques.

Experienced private shippers suggest that collectors employ well-regarded, competent fine-art packers and shippers when valuable objects must be moved. If they are not available, they can be consulted for advice by mail.

Learning to pack safely starts with learning to unpack. When museums receive complex packing units, they make diagrams of exactly how each piece is wrapped, enclosed, and arranged.

Such packing material is kept with the outer wrappings, which are expressly marked. When the exhibition is over, paintings or other objects go back precisely into their own traveling nests.

An advantage of receiving many such units is the exposure to various methods, structures, and materials, in addition to that of seeing the success or failure of the different techniques.

It is recommended that the collector patronize the same truckman and to build a good relationship warmed by tips, as required.

The collector should always be there when packages are unwrapped; it should never be left to others.

Open immediately to check condition. Make claims promptly. Take photographs in wrappings to indicate exactly how the item looked on arrival.

Don't pack (or unpack) when you are tired.

Find and arrange all equipment before you start.

"Bury" fragile objects in wadding or other resilient material.

Be a pessimist; pack against water damage as well as use of the package as a football.

Museums and professionals line boxes with waterproof paper stapled or glued to the box. They also pack individual pieces in sealed waterproof containers.

Small, fragile objects such as ceramics are wrapped in tissue and then cotton to protect the surface, then floated in excelsior in inner cardboard or wooden containers. These in turn are floated in excelsior in a large outer packing box.

If possible, do not pack heavy and light objects in the same container. If they must be packed together, use cross slats to divide the box into compartments.

Inside measurements of boxes must be at least 2¼ inches larger than the largest objects packed in them.

If wooden outer boxes are used, screw box covers into place—never nail them.

Stencil or letter outside of the box with cautionary marks such as "this end up" and "fragile."

Strap or band all boxes being shipped abroad.

Occasionally read a copy of shipping and packing trade magazines for news of latest materials and techniques.

(INSURANCE PROTECTION

The fine points of collection insurance coverage are not within the expertise of the average agent. It is best to consult with an experienced hand in this field.

It is a good idea to have general coverage and the collection insurance handled together, for the client's advantage, so perhaps your friendly insurance agent will call in a consultant for the combined policy.

Antiques, art, and other objects of value to the collector are best separately valued and listed. Most insurance companies offer a "fine arts" policy in connection with a master insurance policy.

Fire insurance rates and theft and burglary rates depend on risk alone, and they are listed according to certain controlled co-ordinates. However, rates for fine arts as well as other scheduled insurance may be more flexible, depending on many circumstances.

It may reduce your premium if the insurance company knows you seldom entertain, your household help has been the same for twenty years, or that you put your most valuable pieces in a vault or warehouse when you go on vacation.

The owner of a policy should become acquainted with the exclusions as well as the coverage. The exclusions are what do you in.

Deductible minimums can be disappointing, and unexpected surprises and depreciation claims are best previewed.

Frequently excluded is breakage, except under limited and stated circumstances. Wear and tear, gradual deterioration, moths, vermin, and damage sustained from repair or restoration are also generally excluded.

Clauses having to do with destruction under customs or quarantine regulations or government confiscation, and those dealing with damage resulting from war or weapons of war give little comfort. Details of flood and storm damage clauses had best be noted too.

You may be well covered for transportation of your collection on a common carrier, but not in a private car.

Note the arrangement in your fine arts policy should the assured and the company fail to agree as to the amount of a loss. This may happen despite the company's acceptance of an appraisal upon which to base the premium.

In the case of disagreement on value, it is customary for each party to select a disinterested and competent appraiser, who submits opinions to an umpire whose decision may be appealed to a court.

Should a total loss for an object be claimed, and there are any remnants, these must usually be turned over to the insurance company.

If the full value of a set is claimed upon the loss of a part, the remaining items in the set must be surrendered.

Pressing claims such as the above are not always to the advantage of the claimant who may be underinsured and figures to make up the difference by salvaging what is left.

Even if the insured has missed a premium payment, the claim for a loss will be paid, say experts. Of course, the company has a counterclaim for the missed premium.

If you take a costly item on memo and the owner says, "Don't worry, it is insured," you should not relax about getting your own insurance to protect yourself. The insurance company will probably pay the owner if you are responsible for the loss or damage, and then turn around and sue you.

To avoid subrogation problems you can get "legal liability insurance" to make sure you are not holding the bag if you have the accident to another's insured property.

If you are making a gift of an object to a museum and taking the tax deduction in segments over a period of years, do you have insurance coverage for the part that still belongs to you? Super-collectors do.

Although to be underinsured is undesirable, especially in the crunch of calamity, overinsurance is no panacea. The insurance company may resist payment of the claim as noted above. Also, at time of death, the insurance figure is likely to be used for estate tax purposes.

CHAPTER 15

CONSERVATION, DISPLAY, AND STORAGE

WHILE A SHOCKED museum director incredulously watched him, Picasso, wanting to show the guest a painting stacked with others in his studio, removed a heavy film of dust with his handkerchief. "That's how I know if anyone has been fiddling with my pictures," he commented. Surely, the artist was in every sense in a position to do as he pleased, but every art collector can only shudder at the thought of that double threat, a layer of dust, and a cloth used for its removal from a canvas.

Neither a damp nor a dry cloth, not even a feather duster (the feathers catch and chip particles of paint), but a very fine soft brush is prescribed for dusting the surface of a painting, and that not too often.

The care and preservation of any kind of collection concerns the potential as well as already involved collector, since few can afford to be as cavalier with their possessions as Picasso, nor equally able, as he was, to literally re-create damaged collections.

⟨ CARE AND PRESERVATION

There are do's and don'ts for the care of just about any object any collector prizes, although occasionally some of these guidelines seem odd or even contradictory. Fortunately, scholarly conservation has recently become an even more important discipline in museum and university research laboratories, and since both are generous with their technology, interested collectors can profit by reading and inquiry.

There are, of course, fine points of restoration best carried out by trained experts. It is generally agreed that more harm than good has been done by amateurs trying to "improve" their treasures by chemical formulac. As the individual collector learns more about caring for a collection, the likelihood of an attempt to supplant experts in repair and restoration becomes more unlikely. However, preservation, proper handling, storage, and display are important activities that the collector can assume more efficiently, having noted professional points.

(RELATIVE HUMIDITY

Much easier to grasp than the theory of relativity and considered much more important to the collector wishing to preserve and protect possessions is the control of relative humidity. This is an equation that represents the proportion of actual moisture in the air to the maximum possible amount at a specific temperature.

Since fibrous materials such as wood, cloth, and paper absorb moisture at high relative humidities and give it off at a low relative humidity, a wide swing from one to the other is particularly destructive to furniture, textiles, paintings, and prints. Other materials are also susceptible, making it essential that collectors of ceramics, enamels, glass, and other materials also be alert to avoid those proportions of humidity in the atmosphere dangerous to their possessions.

Almost every collector is aware that museums control humidity along with temperature and make every effort to avoid the destructive effects of air pollution, but except for supercollectors, not many collectors are aware that a minimum standard of safe relative humidity is not too difficult to achieve in the home, or at least in some part of it.

Experts suggest that a Fahrenheit temperature of 72 degrees in summer with a relative humidity of 55 per cent, and a winter temperature of 68 degrees with a relative humidity of 45 per cent will give adequate general protection. It is more important that it remain constant than that it be set exactly at a particular figure.

The specialist collector may choose to pinpoint or closely approximate the safest figure for a particular category.

- The higher range of relative humidity, about 55 per cent, is most suitable for wood, paintings, ivory, reeds, and leather.
- Paper and plaster prosper best at about 50 per cent.
- Ceramics, especially those with poorly fired or unprotected painted surfaces, require the lower 45 per cent range.
- Metals (which tarnish in high humidity), textiles, and glass are best conserved in the lowest, 40 per cent range of relative humidity.

Relative humidity can be tested by a simple sling psychometer costing a few dollars, or an expensive device costing hundreds. Once a desirable figure has been established, it can be maintained by arranging for water to be released into the atmosphere by electrically powered humidifiers of varying complexity and cost, or by the old-fashioned process of keeping water in containers over radiators as required. Since use of tap water may result in spread of a white film, treated water is recommended.

⟨ HANDLE WITH CARE

Objects are not only endangered in transport, but often also suffer the same fate as people upon the domestic scene, so often the setting for serious accidents. Without giving priority to the inanimate, it must be noted that while minor human hurts often mend without a trace, even slightly damaged possessions have forever lost the sheen or perfection. It becomes imperative for the collector to acquire handling skills and awareness of safety measures, which professionals have acquired by experience and gladly share with collectors.

If the item is small enough, it should be held in the cupped hand.

If the object is large, support by both hands.

Ceramics, glass vessels, and sculpture are never to be picked up by handles, rims, or arms.

Should the object have two parts, several parts, or a separate top, use both hands. Don't ever risk or count on anything being securely attached.

Never push, not even the smallest object. If it has legs, this is the best way to break them. If you are scraping across a surface, you injure both.

All metals including silver, firearms, coins, and sculptural surfaces are best handled with gloves, although a soft cotton cloth will do if the grasp is secure. Fingerprints furnish moisture and oil, which mix poorly with one another and with fine, old, or precious objects.

Neither the front nor the back of a painting is to be touched. A painting is best supported by placing each hand against an opposite edge.

If two are moving a large painting, each should place one hand beneath and the other on the side.

Concerned collectors can and usually do learn to be careful in handling objects, but are at the mercy of guests and visitors whose admiration may be destructive. Signs saying "Handle at your own risk" are hardly suitable for a private home, and the buzzer system that signals a guard that a visitor has come too close to a museum exhibit is somewhat impractical if not downright inhospitable. Automatic howler alarms turned on by touch are intended as protection against burglars, not friends.

Yet the private collector of fragile possessions who makes no effort to defend the collection against handling by thoughtless guests may find that nice guys end up with lots of "as is" items, to say nothing of regrets and losses.

❲ DISPLAY SECURITY

Keeping collections under glass, in locked cabinets, and out of sight solves this problem for some, but the desire to live with and enjoy a collection, as well as to share it, call for such measures as screwing down or bolting objects; fastening loose parts, especially lids, with fine wire; arranging for fragile objects to be placed out of reach or in see-through containers that cannot be touched.

Those collectors who receive strangers in their homes, as is the case with some diplomats, clergy, and certain professionals, have a double purpose in removing the temptation to touch; it can also

be a temptation to take. The wife of a diplomat confides to an insurance agent, "We have to strip the reception rooms of all small
items we can't fasten down."

In general, the vitrine, sometimes of the period, glass case
or cabinet, especially fitted box, holder, or shelf best suited to the
needs of a collection can be discovered by exploring museums and
private sources.

Some collectors solve both their display and storage problems
by arranging with museums to keep their collections on permanent loan, as has been the case with the distinguished collection
of American silver at the Wadsworth Athenaeum, the property of
Philip H. Hammerslough. Both the Hartford, Connecticut, institution and the collector considered themselves mutually fortunate.

⟨ DISPLAY VARIETY

Not only each category, but also specific items that form a collection require particular consideration as to the most attractive, protective, and efficient methods of display (often combined with
storage) in the private home. Fortunately, museum and window
and store display specialists have been inventive in all aspects of
this field, and many of the methods and materials can be adapted
for home use.

Commercial display fixture manufacturers', wholesalers', and
jobbers' catalogs and showrooms present outstanding opportunities for collectors to learn of and to buy useful materials, forms,
holders, and cabinets best suited to their particular needs.

Lighting, a most important aspect of display, requires consideration of the dangerous aspects of light and heat and their deteri-
orating effects. This is not of particular concern to commercial
display professionals; however, it is ever foremost in the thinking
of museum conservationists, whose guidance collectors should follow whenever possible.

Between the supercollector's splendid private gallery, designed
and supervised by professional staff, and the random mixture of
collectibles cached around the household or property of a packrat,
there are many forms of exhibition. How the collection is kept,
and where, depend on the capacity and intentions of its owner as

well as the subject and size. Each situation presents different problems, but the outlook of the owner is a decisive factor.

The collector whose satisfaction is principally in possession will not play the record, wind the toy, or open the fan after acquisition. This type of collector is rarely concerned to share with others and has no interest in domestic display. The collection is less arranged than kept.

Another type is fastidious and organized, also without interest in decorative display, but intent on orderly classification and storage. Here the collection often takes over part of the house, to the futile lamentations of spouse or family.

(ONE AT A TIME

Bowing to the difficulties of space and household limitations, some collectors of butterflies, steins, prints, weathervanes, or porcelains will enthrone a few outstanding examples in a decorative position in the living quarters of the home and more or less neatly keep the body of the collection in available storage space.

Some collectors change their display selections from time to time, depending on season, occasion, or mood, deriving enjoyment from the spotlight (possibly literally) cast on individual pieces and permitting them to be studied in an extra dimension of enjoyment. The advantage of this procedure is that it rotates the stars of the collection for new insights. Also, it is easier to explain to friends and guests the reason for admiration of a few choice pieces than to lecture on many, in the latter instance often boring listeners who could be even more resistant to this than to watching vacation movies.

Even museums show only part of their holdings, and the tendency of late is toward smaller shows, giving the visitor an opportunity to absorb what is offered, rather than to be overwhelmed.

(USING YOUR COLLECTION

There are those lucky collectors who live in original or well-simulated period settings and whose collections are formed to furnish them. For many this is a dream come true after collecting in a particular period and determining to have a living background in which to absorb it. In some cases the house becomes a lived-in museum, a happy circumstance indeed, whether it be Early American, Queen Anne, French Provincial, Louis XIII, elegant Louis XV, or Eastlake Victorian. The eclectic collector, whose acquisitions are the easiest to find, has the greatest difficulty in resisting temptation and separating decoration from collection standards.

Specialist collectors can sometimes shape their collections to their utilitarian needs; silver, rugs, art, and textiles respond well to domestication. Often, storage and display are co-ordinated in one function.

Collections such as baseball cards, where completed series are the goal and items must be kept together, present particular problems. One collector remarked (enviously) of another, "And there are times when he can't even walk around in his house because it's filled with cards. Honest to God, you can't even open the front door all the way." Since baseball cards are conventionally kept in cigar and shoe boxes, this collector who has more than ten million cards, needs a lot of them.

(EXHIBITION TECHNIQUES

Study collections, whether of locks, keys, or laces, require easy accessibility, but must be stored in well-defined classifications. If well recorded and cataloged, items can be removed for display and easily recovered and replaced by use of the accession number, which provides the key to its location.

An extraordinary installation at the Yale University Art Gallery, entitled "American Arts and the American Experience," basically a teaching exhibition, brought forward many objects that had been sequestered in storage areas. Unveiled in 1973, it has continued to influence private collectors as well as museums, because with a minimum of space, the display handsomely shows a maximum of objects, intelligently integrated.

A single display, devoted to ten Windsor chairs of the eighteenth and early nineteenth centuries, shows eight chairs attached to the wall of the room enclosure, with just two on the floor of the small required area. Thus the undersides and back, important areas of workmanship, are shown along with variety of design, clearly outlined in an attractive, intrinsically decorative display, with the essential shapes of the chairs forming eye-catching patterns.

Carved seventeenth-century chests, displayed in tiers, offer opportunity for study from many angles without having to be moved. Heavier objects set on raised platforms of varying heights and collections of smaller items, silver, and iron are hung on walls in interesting design-related arrangements. In some cases they are similar to catalog layout fashion pages.

Thus large numbers of objects in small space allow for careful examination of each piece, all in the framework of an over-all appealing decorative treatment. The mazelike displays simulate small rooms, all painted white, as are cases and bases, bringing out the forms to full advantage and especially are suitable to the simplicity and strength of strong forms.

The adaptation of objects to uses other than their original purposes has never appealed to serious collectors; as a matter of fact, most abhor it. Specialist dealers will not knowingly sell rare collectibles for purposes of transformation, and many discerning generalist dealers also warn against it.

However, vintage ice boxes turned into contemporary bars upset no one, and Victorian salt boxes used as well planters raise no cries of vandalism. Both taste and judgment are factors in this area of collecting display. In general, if no permanent change from the original state is required, and the use or display does not cause the item to deteriorate, the collector may follow good conscience consistent with acceptance of a caretaker's role in the formation and passing on of any collection.

Conservators say that placement in the household can damage; some areas should be avoided.

No pictures or art objects to be placed over a fireplace that is in use. Heat and possible smoke damage are feared.

The sweating walls of a basement prophesy mildew and its attendant disasters. It may take a while, but all that moisture will do its harm. Electric bulbs, heaters, and fans are used to fight it.

It may be tempting to keep some of your folk art in the kitchen, but that fine deposit of grease won't act as a beauty cream.

Paintings are seldom hung in the bath, but graphics often are. All that steam will help them go down the drain.

Large glass windows or walls subject your collection to extreme swings of temperature and relative humidity, unless countervened.

Avoid proximity to air conditioners and radiators for collections that include paintings, graphics, ivory, wood in any form, or textiles.

⟨ STORAGE PRECAUTIONS

It is easy to believe that just because something has been stored, packed away, or placed out of reach, its safety is assured. Unfortunately, improperly stored collections can quietly deteriorate, noisily disintegrate, or otherwise succumb to dangers the collector had not sufficient foresight to prevent.

The collector as custodian and caretaker has a responsibility not only to the collection as property of value, but also as cultural heritage. Accidents may happen, but those who have taken sufficient precautions should have less of them to regret.

Display and storage areas for collections are often equipped with metal shelves in the belief they are preferable and safer in case of fire. This is not necessarily so.

Uninsulated metal is the best and fastest heat conductor, and unless a fire is retarded by suitable insulation, its fury may be more destructive at a higher heat level.

Some museum authorities believe that paper, ceramics, glass, and textiles would suffer less damage in a tightly enclosed wooden cabinet, even if the exterior were scorched by fire, than within a case of uninsulated metal.

There is another disadvantage of metal shelves, due to lack of surface resilience, so that even gently setting down pottery, porcelain, or glass may result in damage, and a slip or fall in disaster.

Felt-covered shelves are recommended, to add a degree of safety.

Condensation of moisture on metal surfaces is considered another hazard.

Adjustable and interchangeable shelves, permitting arrangement to allow for clearance of objects stored, are desirable.

Wooden trays, preferably padded, are excellent safeguards for smaller items. If an object should fall, it would remain in the tray, always kept underneath when material is handled or moved.

Small objects can be sealed in individual see-through bags.

Unframed drawings, autographs, or paper documents may be kept visible when covered with glassine paper, with hinged mats as window fronts.

Some collectors make their own boxes with hollowed areas to exactly fit the piece, in the Chinese style. These can also be custom-ordered. Any means by which abrasion can be avoided is worth considering.

Don't keep musical instruments in "dead" storage. They require a ventilated atmosphere.

If you are storing fine wood furniture, keep it on platforms in ventilated rooms. Cover with muslin or with heavy paper, but make sure the paper is fitted neatly at the corners.

Shelves for glass and small ceramics should be narrow enough to allow easy viewing and for objects to be reached without disturbing adjacent ones.

Sliding doors with screened or glass windows are recommended.

Laces and linens are best rolled. Blue tissue paper helps to prevent discoloration.

Tar paper is a no-no for storing textiles. High temperatures and parachlorobenzine melt or dissolve the tar, and can cause serious damage.

Kraft paper over tissue paper serves as a good dust protector for textiles. They need ventilation, yet require protection from light.

Textiles are stored with parachlorobenzine crystals as protection against mildew, mold, and insects. If it is not possible to enclose the material with solid crystals, museums use commercial sprays.

Rugs and textiles need a rest period from any position in which they are stored. This is true if they are rolled, hung, or folded. Flat is best, but seldom practical.

Tapestries are seldom small enough to be stored flat. If they are folded, it is urged that the first folds be kept parallel to the warp threads. When the piece is hung for display, the folds will be horizontal and the weight of the fabric will uncrease them in a few days. Vertical folds are never erased by hanging.

If silver cannot be kept in cabinets or containers lined with tarnish-resistant cloth, squares of camphor in closed cabinets will slow the tarnishing process.

Metal parts of arms, armor, and many other base metals are treated with neutral shoe polish by museums that have found that oil is too gummy and easily rubs off.

Dry, cracked wood can be restored by immersion in beeswax, but it is a tricky process, one for experts. Feed your wood before it requires emergency treatment.

Large, unframed prints, watercolors, and documents, are best kept in oversize portfolios. Standard sizes go into solander boxes and portfolios that fit on shelves.

Whenever possible, tall cabinets should be fitted with pull-out shelves, so material taken out can be rested thereon as it is taken down.

When prints, watercolors, and photographs are out of their permanent cases or portfolios, they should be kept in what are called "handling mats," which are folders of lightweight rag content.

Keep anything but rag paper away from all paper collectibles. The acid content in other paper causes deterioration. Newspapers are anathema for storage and packing in connection with any other paper.

Tiny splits in fabrics, paper, bone, or leather may result from mechanical stress, which can be stopped and further weakening arrested if traced.

Professionals fumigate paper materials of all sorts in thymol chambers to prevent fungus growth and foxing stains.

Don't use any cleaner or chemical unless you know its properties. If it spills on some material other than the one on which it can be safely used, be prepared to remove by correct means.

All light must be considered a potential source of deterioration and used only with safeguards. Sunlight is especially destructive to many materials.

Heat above 72 degrees Fahrenheit is generally unhealthy for collections.

Polluted air, especially with sulphur content, can destroy even bronze and iron. Dust is also an enemy.

Drafts are not good either. Wood and leather are especially susceptible to them, say conservators.

CHAPTER **16**

SURVIVAL OR THE FINAL RITES OF SELLING

FOR CERTAIN INDIVIDUALS, the moment a collection has been completed, it's as though a balloon were pricked and all the air let out. No longer buoyed by the excitement of having a creative purpose, they lose interest, usually a prelude to selling, dismantling, or sometimes donating the results of an endeavor that may have taken years to achieve. Yet having terminated one, such a person may immediately begin to form yet another collection.

⟮ FINISHING TOUCHES

Dealers tell of collectors who make it a point to avoid this letdown by indefinitely postponing the crisis of conclusion. Even when collecting a closed series, it is possible to defer completion by searching for ever more perfect examples of each specimen that has been acquired in the past. When there is no framework of series, it is always possible to enlarge, enrich, refine, and follow unfulfilled aspirations that permanently elude the grasp.

Of course, collectors with such psychological quirks are in the minority. Most need raise no artificial obstacles, but find a sufficiency of real barriers to formation of the perfect, finished collection. The collector's grip on acquired treasures is more often loosened by exterior forces, although occasionally altered tastes will dictate dissolution of a collection. Death, taxes, different life styles, and economic choice or necessity are usually responsible when a collection changes hands, sometimes finding a place intact under an institutional or private roof, or most often dismembered and scattered in the marketplace.

⟮ HANGING ON

Mindful that shrouds have no pockets, collectors determined that the collections they must leave behind continue as an embodiment of their personalities and identities, come up with fascinating and ingenious methods to achieve leaving themselves behind, as an alternative to taking the collection along.

This makes museum directors and trustees unhappy, and often

they feel they must renounce bequests making stringent demands. Collections that may never be altered in any fashion, neither added to or subtracted from; requirements that the entirety be exhibited together in galleries of certain size; directions for naming museums or parts thereof, even when accompanied by trusts to pay for following the will or whims of the late donors, are often grudgingly followed, even if accepted.

When Samuel Pepys left his library to Magdalen College at Cambridge University, his will required that every book be placed as it was on his shelves. Since Trinity College was named as the alternative recipient should Magdalen College fail to carry out these instructions, it may be said that even from his grave, the dead hand of Samuel Pepys still arranges his books. Reportedly, Trinity checks annually to see that every book is where it belongs, still hoping to press its claim!

The handsome $7 million Lehman Wing of the Metropolitan Museum of Art was decreed by the will of the collector to include exact replicas of the rooms in which the paintings and art objects were displayed in his home. Though some critics find year 1905 "Renaissance" room settings detract from the great art, and some say the scale of the whole pavilion diminishes as it overwhelms, the grandeur of the gift was persuasive to museum authorities.

⟮ GIVING CAN BE BETTER

Comparatively few collectors in the lower and midreaches of affluence take advantage of United States laws by which gifts of antiques, art, and collectibles, as well as other categories, to religious, educational, scientific, literary, and charitable organizations properly qualified, are encouraged by allowing for deduction on income-tax returns to the extent of some percentage of the whole sum due.

Obviously favoring the wealthy in high brackets, this procedure is not without value in medium and low ranges. A most attractive aspect is the valuation at "fair market value" at the time of the gift, often much greater than its original cost at the time of purchase. Since the figure is most often reckoned at retail, it is generally more than the collector could get for the item by selling it to a dealer. In addition, collectors finding themselves short of cash with which to pay taxes, or when philantropically inclined, can look to their possessions and then to willing and grateful recipient institutions for some relief.

⟨ DEATH AND TAXES

Problems arising from the inflated or otherwise greater value of collections, works and objects of art, and antiques, which bring estates into higher tax brackets, are reverse aspects of the advantages of collecting, unless provision is made in advance.

Collections must sometimes be sold to pay these unexpectedly high taxes, although the heirs would prefer to keep them or possibly to sell at a more opportune time than that presenting itself when the taxes are due. To avoid this, some collectors preplan by making insurance policies payable directly to the estate, producing cash for tax payments or arranging for cash to be available from savings. Another method, favored by supercollectors, is the purchase of a type of government bond called "cemetery bonds" or "flower bonds." These bonds can be bought at a discount and are accepted by the government at face value for the payment of estate taxes. No longer issued, such bonds offer a chance for the estate to enjoy the liquidity that avoids selling off other assets.

⟨ SELLING OFF

Despite the lures of immortality or monetary advantages of making bequests or lifetime gifts, liquidation of collections by selling remains a common and necessary procedure that may be marked with grief or relief, but usually has some overtones of sadness, whether or not the collector survives to see it.

However the decision to sell is made, few are prepared for the trauma of selling. Without experience in having sold private possessions, many lose the advantage of having formed a collection because they don't know the techniques of disposition or the realities of the marketplace. Those who have traded and sold while forming their collections are the best equipped, whether hard-nosed supercollectors of masterpieces, modest middlecollectors, or innovative crazycollectors. In any case, all collectors can profit by an advance survey of the role of seller in which they are pitted against the well-honed skills of dealers, auctioneers, and even some crafty collectors.

❰ APPRAISE ALL YOUR OPTIONS

The options for liquidating a collection for cash include disposal at auction, selling to dealers of various strata, consignment to dealers, and selling to private individuals or institutions, possibly museums or corporations.

Before you come to grips with the decisions that will determine whether you or someone else reaps the material profits from the values that have been accumulated in your collection, you must consider some important steps.

If you were trapped with some items of questionable authenticity that pull down the over-all standard of your collection, get rid of them separately. It is true that this sort of thing gets sloughed off with famous-name collections, but it's dangerous for lesser ones.

If you are selling the collection for someone incapacitated or deceased, look for plans for liquidation among the effects.

The whole collection should be listed and described—if possible from what are now its invaluable inventory records.

If neither inventory, insurance policies, nor other sources show updated valuations, and the seller is not equipped to establish them, find a competent, disinterested appraiser, experienced in valuing the objects under consideration.

Dealers and auctioneers are usually professional appraisers; be sure you get someone who does not expect to buy the collection cheap as a result of appraising under true value.

Appraisers' fees are flexible; discuss them in advance. The greater the number of items and their value, the lower the fee in terms of percentage.

Before inviting buyers to view, or transporting any part of the collection, make certain it is sufficiently insured against possible hazards. Short-term insurance is not costly, and objects that have survived for hundreds of years may now be in peril.

Key pieces will often carry along items that have importance only in relation to them, and little value without them. Hang on to everything until you have been reliably briefed.

Don't be guided by the original cost of an object. Consider its current retail market value in relation to your marketing procedure.

The element of timing plays a part in successful liquidation, with a good general economy an optimal condition, not always available.

Dealers advertise and auctioneers arrange sales to coincide with exhibitions, shows, and conventions. The private collector wishing to dispose of a collection will also watch for scheduled events with an eye to making the most of them.

(AUCTION SELLING

There are so many gradations of auction firms below the top that the consignee had best determine the reliability as well as the capability of the auctioneers in living up to expectations based on their estimates.

Check out the reputation of auction firms by talking with some of their clients.

Don't put your fine collection in a sale with a lot of junk that will not attract the kind of trade willing or able to pay good prices for yours.

On the other hand, those auction firms that handle only costlier, quality material would not have the public for more modest or certain specialized collections. However, if you go to the best, they will recommend others. It may not work that way in reverse.

The trade considers that on the average, auction prices fall midway between retail and wholesale.

When considering a sale at auction, note that auctioneers' rates can be flexible. They will bend them for very desirable collections or if business is slow. Try for the best terms you can get.

Read the fine print in an auction contract. Percentage of commission is usually based per lot or per item. It grows less as the individual figure rises, but that doesn't do you any good on the overall amount.

If the sale is held on your own premises, don't discount the mess or upset involved.

If you are to be charged for transportation, packing, shipping, insurance, photographs, the catalog, repairs, or other auction expenses, have them spelled out in advance and limited.

Establish a reserve price below which the item will not be sold at the auction. Determine what charge the auctioneer will or will not make in this event.

Be sure you have a copy in writing of the reserve price for each item as agreed upon between you and the auctioneer.

The reserve price is your only protection against the "ring" consisting of dealers who bid together as a group and later repeat the auction for themselves, splitting the difference.

Settle the date of sale and payment in the contract.

Make sure it is the auctioneer who is responsible for paying you, not the buyers.

Attend the sale, if at all possible.

Keep in mind, when negotiating for an auction sale, that you do not receive the price bid paid by the buyer, but possibly about three quarters of it.

❨ SELLING TO DEALERS

When negotiating with dealers, the collector will rarely be offered a price to begin. They insist the seller set a price, in the hope that the true value will be underestimated.

Dealers will usually pay up to about half of what they expect to get for desirable stock. If quick turnover is assured, they will pay more than half, but fight you all the way up.

Don't be taken in by the offer of a remarkably high price for a single item or a few items, far beyond what you know the true value to be. This is an old trick to get you to believe that the generous buyer who gives you fifty dollars for an item worth five, is not taking advantage of you when offering you practically nothing for the rest.

Complex offers to buy part now, with a contract to buy more later, deferred payments, and similar complicated contracts should only be considered with the advice of lawyers.

Offers to take your collection to sell on consignment should be weighed carefully. In general, it isn't as good an idea for the seller as for the consignee, who has merchandise to sell without making any investment.

The collector who has been buying largely on the advice of a specialist dealer over a period of many years will find that as a rule such a dealer will make an offer for the entire collection. Although it may seem a good offer, check it out against others.

Don't spend money refurbishing or reconditioning if you expect to sell to dealers. They can have it done for less and won't include your cost in the price paid to you.

Don't include your address when you advertise. A blind box number is safer and gives you a chance to check the inquirer's bona fides.

(ALTERNATIVE DISPOSAL

Corporations forming collections may be potential buyers for yours. If you believe you have something of interest to one, write to the president of the company. If there is a curator or officer in charge of the collection, you will be referred to that individual.

Museums occasionally buy from private collectors. If you think your collection or part of it may be of interest, write to the head of that department.

Modest collections can be liquidated at fleamarkets by those with a flair for selling. But have a partner to help you watch your merchandise and spell you.

Collectors often open shops to sell their lifetime collections and accumulations. This may peter out when the original merchandise is gone, but sometimes is the start of a new and successful career. If the investment can be controlled along with the overhead, figure in some salary as well.

(THE TOUCHSTONE OF SUCCESS

Whether or not a collection endures, its very formation is an act of creation, and its existence, even if temporary, touches not only the collector but also those who have been exposed to it.

There are many standards for judging collections, but the measure above all that validates the time, energy, and money that has gone into one is the degree to which it arouses wonder. It is wonder, that marvelous stretching of the imagination, enriching our understanding and giving us greater emotional capacity as well as intellectual stimulation, that is the touchstone of success for every collection.

CHAPTER **17**

COLLECTORS' GRAPEVINE AND MISCELLANY

⟨ HOW TO FORM A COLLECTION
WITHOUT MONEY
⟨ COLLECTORS' COMMENTARY

THE ABSENCE OF money in forming a collection especially interests those whose condition can be described as *sans argent*; certainly they cannot be faulted for wishing to participate in such a satisfying activity. Often embarrassed to inquire directly, they sometimes attempt to query collectors or dealers, but usually in such a manner that the question is obscured, even if answers should be available. Here are some suggestions.

❲ HOW TO FORM A COLLECTION WITHOUT MONEY

Go into a field in which discards and free items predominate.

Beer cans, calendars, autographs, shopping bags, advertising post cards, match covers and autographs, and candy wrappers, as well as shells, stones, "found" art objects, and bottles are good bets.

Bottle collectors start by looking through their own households and move on to digging in dumps. Autograph collectors who beg for celebrity autographs will swap them and then build to more worthwhile specialties by writing letters to entice replies.

Offer to clean out cellars, garages, and attics for some of the collectible contents. Old photographs may be especially fruitful for burgeoning collectors.

If nothing you possess meets the guidelines in Chapter 4, take something you already own but don't want, and either sell or trade for something you would like to collect.

Get a part-time job with a second-hand dealer and swap your services for merchandise that is suitable for your collection or can be sold or exchanged.

Spend a lot of time in the public library reading about the subject you have decided to collect. Ask the librarian to subscribe to collectors' periodicals of interest to you.

Beat the garbage truck on its rounds by a few hours. Junk and second-hand dealers have been known to make such pickups to good advantage.

Go to fleamarkets with your culls and duplicates. Get there early and sell to others or trade with them.

Advertise on your school, supermart, club, library, or pastoral billboard with the possibility of offering services for the object of your inquiry.

Lavatory graffiti, if unusual, as well as more public forms, gravestone epitaphs, jump rope rhymes, and found objects are illustrations of "freebie" collectibles.

The French term *bricoleur* refers to a person who prefers to recycle or rearrange what already exists, rather than to utilize new raw materials. As the latter become more precious, with scarcity and consumption working against each other, the utility of potential as well as existing antiques will become greater value factors. This has been the case with Franklin stoves.

There's a kind of trivia known in the trade as "real garbage," meaning that only the buyer values it. This is known as brummagem by some who prefer a more elegant term. Start with this, everybody has some of it. You can trade it.

Just as there are photograph safaris in which the purpose of the hunt is to photograph the wild animals, so there are beginning to be areas of collecting in which the photographic record of the object is sought. Baroque European doorways, Early American and Victorian gravestones, unusual fountains, and Art Deco building façades are among these.

A historical viewpoint helps many in the early choice of subjects that will form collections of interest in the future. Others have an anthropologist's view of our own culture. Marijuana-connected artifacts and other counterculture material are already in the collecting sights of some crystal gazers.

Use of electronic tape to transfer American gospel, jazz, folk, historical opera, and other classical and popular music from records brings a new dimension into this field of collecting.

If you are annoyed at having to pay a toll over a bridge or buy an extra token, you may find that it more than compensates for your trouble. Collectors who specialize in transportation tokens are called vecturists; bridge toll tokens are the oldest type.

A collector of political campaign buttons observes that half of Goldwater's votes came from button collectors. Now the hobby has attracted many young people who aren't at all conservative.

What was a generation of rejecters in the 1960s became a generation of collectors in the following decade.

Samuel Goldwyn said, "If I want to send a message, I'll send a telegram," but someone might have told him that collections often proclaim activist and ideological convictions. Women's liberation, union history, black culture, and Indian justice have inspired collections that are creative propaganda.

Most stock certificates strike their owners as beautiful, but those of defunct companies or otherwise worthless in face value, are especially collected for the appeal of their ornate engraving and printing. Viewed as old documents, they are rising in price.

A sampling of items as they are listed in the "Wanted" columns of collectors' popular periodicals may be only the top of the iceberg, but it does indicate some trends of interest to hopeful if somewhat indigent collectors.

Alaska Klondike items
Antiques of commerce
    catalogs
    office equipment
    signs
    store fixtures

Anything on magic and witchcraft
Architectural gingerbread
Authentic Mickey Mouse items
Bawdyhouse tokens
Beaded glass fringe
Bed-, foot-, and handwarmers
Black Americana
Calligraphy examples and equipment
Cap pistols
Early bathtubs
Early motorcycles
Early Sears, Roebuck catalogs
Early Sears, Roebuck merchandise
Egg baskets and wire items
Electrical and scientific
   electric light bulbs
   early radio and TV
   wireless items
   insulators
   telephones
"Hate Roosevelt" material
Kate Greenaway almanacs
Letter clips and letter hooks
Lithophanes
Medical ephemera
Movie stars' photos taken before 1950
Old china fish sets
Old fishing reels
Old park and railroad station benches
Old spectacles and lorgnettes
Old straight razors
Old string holders
Old travel booklets
Planters' peanut jars and lids
Pot lids
Radio giveaway premiums
Refillable fountain pens
Steamboat items

Stereoscopes and kaleidoscopes
Trucks and tractors made before 1930
Vintage ladies' and men's hats
Watch stands and ring trees
Zeppelin items

⟨ COLLECTORS' COMMENTARY

When a dealer tells the newspapers he has discovered a two-hundred-thousand-dollar painting in an antique or junk shop for a few hundred dollars, you can be sure it is "not for sale." When it really happens, they don't talk and they do sell.

Some thrift shop habitué collectors have refined their coverage to the point where they make their rounds when they know their contacts are on the job.

Commercial fund-raising art and antique auctions and sales are often run under the auspices of a charity that gets a percentage of the "take." This permits buyers to make out their checks to the charity with the hope that the whole amount can be taken as a tax deduction.

Ninety per cent of art sales are made privately, according to some market authorities. Obviously, these can't be included in price guide information.

A supercollector gave a museum a painting that its press releases announced had cost $1.4 million. Actually, it had been acquired through swapping items that had cost much less, but the higher the price claimed, the greater the hoped-for size of the donor's tax deduction.

There's something about the antiques business that attracts independent spirits. An advertisement for daguerreotypes, placed in a trade publication, closed with the postscript, "If you are a hunter or trap user, lose this ad. I will not deal with you."

It is normal for artists making graphics to pull a few artist's proofs, and these appeal to collectors. Lately, it has been noted that some graphics appear on the market with large numbers marked "E.A.," the initials indicating *épreuve artiste*. Insiders suggest that this greedy practice will eventually catch up with the market and reduce the value of these items.

Nixon and Agnew supporters may have something besides disappointment if they hold on to their autographs and other memorabilia, including political mementos. The rarer items are considered good bets for the future.

Running out of space to store his own classic cars, a Chicago collector opened a historical antique auto museum, only to be besieged by other car collectors to exhibit their rarities on his burglarproof premises. Large numbers of collectors hide their valuable vintage cars, afraid of theft.

When it appeared that wealthy Iranians were paying record prices for Persian antiquities, a network alert went off all over the world as dealers and auctioneers sought this material. A collector who had intended to give his Middle Eastern ceramic and bronze collection to a museum was persuaded to auction it. When critic John Russel said that revivals of forgotten art are never unmotivated, he spoke truly.

There was an English book collector in the eighteenth century who had his coffin made from his bookshelves.

It is said that people who collect antique hymnals often steal them from churches.

Collecting islands off the coast of Maine is the fancy of Mrs. David Rockefeller, according to her former daughter-in-law.

A dealer reports that one of his customers will buy anything that has been repaired in an interesting, artful, or unusual fashion. He literally collects the technique of repair, rather than the object.

There's an ad that occasionally appears in a collectors' publication, searching for old chicken coops and privies. They won't say what for.

The National Canadian Pacific Railroad opened its own antiques shops to sell railroadiana. One collector bought ten locomotive plates at seventy-five dollars each, together with photographs of the original engines.

It was easier to be a collector in the mid-seventeenth century, when London bibliophile Narcissus Lutrell could buy everything published in London in his time, from common political tracts peddled on the street for a penny, to masterpieces of poetry in fine editions with modest means.

Shell collectors who documented where each shell was taken were able to aid the Navy during World War II when invasions of remote Pacific islands required information on the shelving of beaches, depth of waters, and currents.

Sometimes the ugliest antique or vintage toys and dolls are the rarest and highest priced. They didn't sell well, and few were made.

An almost certain dividend in developing a line of inquiry in collecting is that quite suddenly, what had never previously been noted, crops up in all directions.

Collectors not wishing to see the spotlight focus on what they are collecting, will, like one, finding the NRA Depression stamp on a box of brass washers in an old hardware store, buy the contents of the box in order to get the container.

Individuals forced to part with collections for reasons beyond their control will often substitute auction catalogs or photographs of the collection as treasured possessions.

Collectors love being courted by museums, even though the collectors know they aren't loved for themselves alone. In return, they dangle and tease. Great collectors have affairs with important institutions; some foxy modest collectors enjoy being wooed by lesser ones.

Sometimes it takes a while for lightning that struck to take effect. B. G. Cantor started his fabulous collection of Rodin's works two years after seeing the "Hand of God" sculpture that set him off.

A collector of Roseville pottery, the ware made in Zanesville, Ohio, from the 1890s to the 1950s, spent one vacation traveling across the United States, not only searching out items for his collection, but also keeping a record of the variety and prices of the over five thousand pieces that he sighted. He found the price structure very uneven, prices for the same item varying by as much as 50 per cent.

Genealogy, the study of family history, is popular with Americans of all backgrounds, but particularly with those whose roots are in Britain. Several hundred firms there are in the business of tracing family relationships for a fee. It is reported that Americans are the most assiduous seekers, hoping for stately if not noble connections, but most often ending up with smaller fry, such as farmers and tradesmen.

Thieves spurned other valuables and jewelry, making off with a collector's sports cards worth seven thousand dollars, including a leaf gum company set worth twenty to fifty dollars per card.

A dealer in limited-edition ceramics sends his customers post cards from his yachting trips with the greeting, "So long, sucker."

Preferring to avoid the now commercialized term "limited edition," the art world now uses "multiples" to describe works that are produced in more than a single offering. Each is supposed to be signed and an original work.

The Detroit Museum of Art has imbued T-shirt collectors with confidence, by an exhibition of two hundred decorated T-shirts offered as a contemporary art form.

Dependence on signature may boomerang. The signature may be missing and the work authentic. Picasso wanted to sign a number of his early works that he had given to his former mistress and mother of his daughter. However, his wife Jacqueline jealously forbade him to do so, and he deferred to her. The 129 works were later offered in Geneva, having been sold by Marie Therese Walter to an internationally reputable gallery for less than she had hoped to receive.

Gallery and auction glamour leave canny collectors cold. They are not impressed by fancy frames, picture lights, or name plates.

If you have ever been part of or even witnessed an ugly emotional row about how best to fairly divide family heirlooms, you will appreciate the desirability of avoiding such a situation. Of course, if the deceased had made the decisions by will, or even an informal list, there would be no problem, but people too often postpone such intentions indefinitely. There is no pat solution to this age-old source of dissension, but experts suggest several methods that may avoid acrimony, or what is even worse, costly legal battles.

- Draw for the items in question by lot. No one will be happy, but accusations will be fewer.
- Sell the object in question; exactly divide the proceeds.
- Hold a private family auction; give the money to the deceased's favorite charity.

There is a specimen known as the trader rat, which always leaves something in return for what it removes. Some people trade so much, they never form a collection either.

Not even great artists form flawless collections. A few of the non-Picassos in Picasso's collection were not considered worthy of hanging in the Louvre.

Collectors can only respond with sheer envy when they learn that a peerless collection of Scythian gold objects that date as early as 3000 B.C. and are mentioned by Herodotus were the gift of a

Russian mine owner to Peter the Great. Having to buy just doesn't compare to receiving treasures as gifts.

You may choose to collect alone, jointly with a friend or marital partner, even with a child. Some find the solo search more fruitful; others prefer teamwork. They say two can hunt more thoroughly than one—repair, restore and clean, even pay better than one. Great collecting marriages are made in heaven, but hell has nothing on them if they break up.

Although the Duveen family had been antiques and art dealers for several generations, no member was permitted to form a personal collection, on the principle that the dealer who competes with clients cannot keep his priorities straight.

They tell of a London dealer in engravings who came into a fortune. He locked his doors, never sold another print, and enjoyed his treasures like a miser.

Some of those record prices fetched at auction for seemingly outlandish items are paid by decorators for the restaurant trade, by specialists who rent out for window and shop displays, and by operators of commercial museums.

Surpassing stamps and coins in popularity, one of the most widespread items collected in the U.S.S.R. is the souvenir lapel emblem, called *znachki*. Despite government disapproval, largely because of use of raw materials, collectors meet surreptitiously to swap, buy, and compare high-priced rarities.

When trying to dispose of limited-edition items, write to the producer and ask for a list of dealers specializing in each issue, then send a copy of your inventory list to these outlets.

There is a special courtesy among collectors that precludes the use of the term "fake" in referring to another collector's possession in his or her presence. This is the same delicacy of feeling that keeps people from telling parents their children are bastards.

Bowling Green State University in Ohio publishes the *Journal of Popular Culture* and gives both B.A. and M.A. degrees in popular culture, including study of comic-book and record collecting. The department has six hundred undergraduates and hopes for more as it grows.

⟨ ABOUT THE AUTHOR

SYLVIA O'NEILL DORN has been antiques and collecting feature writer for McCall's *Better Living* magazine, editor of *Giftwares* magazine, and is author of the book *The Insider's Guide to Antiques, Art and Collectibles*. Her lifelong involvement in the world of collecting includes posts as antiques buyer for leading department stores. She was scriptwriter for the TV program "What's New in Collecting" and a lecturer at New York University's School for Adult Education. She thinks her early interest in collecting originated in a childhood fascination with objects that had a family history. She lives in New York City, and she travels in the United States and abroad to lecture on collecting and to visit fleamarkets, auctions, shows, exhibitions, shops, galleries, museums, and private collections. She is a graduate of the University of Cincinnati.